Jackie R. Matende
Home Library.

I Want My Church to Grow

I Want My Church to Grow

C. B. HOGUE

BROADMAN PRESS   Nashville, Tennessee

Dewey Decimal Classification: 269
Subject headings: EVANGELISTIC WORK//CHURCHES

All Scripture quotations, unless otherwise indicated, are from the Revised Standard Version.

Scripture quotations marked "NASB" are from the *New American Standard Bible.* © The Lockman Foundation, La Habra, California, 1971. Published by Creation House, Inc., Carol Stream, Illinois.

Scripture quotations marked "TLB" are taken from *The Living Bible, Paraphrased* (Wheaton: Tyndale House Publishers, 1971) and are used by permission.

Scripture quotations marked "TEV" are taken from the *Today's English Version* of the New Testament. Copyright © American Bible Society 1966, 1971.

Library of Congress Catalog Card Number: 77-85280
Printed in the United States of America.

Dedicated to
my ministering sons:
Robert, Randy, Rodney, and Ronald

Foreword

This is a book for the times.

The times—the end of the 1970s and the beginning of the 1980s—are times for unprecedented effectiveness in evangelism and church growth in America. Rarely in the history of our nation have the American people been as hungry for God as they are now. Church attendance is on the upswing. Religion is a popular topic of conversation in factories, on street corners, and among students on college campuses. Many are now asking what it means to be "born again," and are wondering out loud whether it is an option for them.

The harvest is ripe. God's Spirit has opened multitudes of hearts. But no harvest reaps itself. We are commanded to pray that the Lord of the harvest will send laborers out into the harvest field (Matt. 9:38). And the harvesters who go need the best of tools if they are going to be effective reapers.

C. B. Hogue's book is a much-needed tool for this task. It is a manual that gets it all together. It is a superb book on evangelism by one of the nation's big league evangelism executives. But it is not just another good book on evangelism. The evangelism that Hogue proposes here is not the kind that is satisfied with mere decisions for Christ. Beyond that it seeks true discipleship and expects those who respond to be responsible members of churches. Thus, it is a book on church growth and a worthy addition to the growing body of literature in the field.

Hogue's underlying theme is "bold evangelism." This thread ties together exciting case studies of rapidly growing churches in Arizona, Tennessee, Oklahoma, Nebraska,

Florida, Mississippi, Louisiana, Maryland, and California. The theme is woven throughout valuable sections analyzing the principles of church growth and drawing from a wide selection of contemporary literature on the subject. It guides the formulation of practical suggestions for the local church, including how-to-do-it forms that you can start using for your own church immediately.

If you are a pastor or a lay person, and if you have ever said, "I want my church to grow," read this book. It will broaden your horizons. It will warm your heart. It will lift your spirits. It will challenge you to action for the glory of God.

I commend this book so highly because it throbs with the heartbeat of God: His desire that the lost sheep be found and returned to their Father's fold. In our time two of every three American adults need to be evangelized. *I Want My Church To Grow* is destined to make a substantial contribution to that task because it is truly a book for these times.

C. Peter Wagner
Fuller Seminary School of World Mission
Pasadena, California

Contents

News Item 1

JERUSALEM—Roman and Jewish authorities have divided over how to handle the burgeoning "Christian church" movement, reliable sources confirmed here today.

Roman officials have decided merely to "monitor" events, believing "this is not yet a political problem," said a spokesman for the administration. "We have nothing to worry about at this time," the spokesman confided. "The movement—if you want to call it that—seems centered in Jerusalem and is definitely not, at this time, a threat to our government."

In a palace briefing, administration officials declined to describe the steps in the monitoring process, but admitted recent reports of "mass conversions to this Christian faith" did cause concern in the inner circles of Procurator Pontius Pilate and Jewish King Herod Antipas.

Jewish religious leaders, however, are reacting heatedly to claims by the fledgling church that its leader is "the Messiah, the king promised by God to his people."

In the weeks since the death of the movement's leader—an obscure Galilean named Jesus—more than 10,000 persons have reportedly affiliated with the Christian organization.

Some 3,000 people joined following a dramatic appeal by Simon Peter, spokesman for the church group. Several days later, 5,000 men answered a second appeal by Peter.

Reacting to the growing attention the group was receiving, Jewish leaders arrested Peter and John, an associate.

In a stormy session before the Sanhedrin council, Peter and John were instructed to cease "speaking or teaching in the name of Jesus."

The two rejected the demand, arguing "we cannot stop speaking of what we ourselves have seen and heard."

Unable to substantiate charges of subversion, the two were released on their own recognizance. However, as reports of "miracles and continued preaching" reached the Jewish religious leaders, Peter and John were again arrested.

This time the pair escaped, returning to the Temple where they resumed their fiery appeals to the people to "accept the new life in Jesus Christ."

Angered by the two "Jesus-ites" refusal to accept the verdict of the council, council authorities arrested the pair for a third time.

Speaking for the council, the high priest shouted, "We gave strict orders not to teach in the name of this man (Jesus). But see what you've done! You've spread your teaching all over Jerusalem, and you want to make us responsible for his death!"

Peter, defending the church group, insisted, "You killed him by nailing him to a cross. And God raised him to his right side as Leader and Savior, to give to the people of Israel the opportunity to repent and have their sins forgiven. We are witnesses to these things."

Tempers flared as other angry shouts were exchanged, reported an observer, but violence—including threats to "put the apostles to death"—was averted when Gamaliel, a highly respected Pharisee, gained control of the council meeting.

After ordering Peter and John taken out of the room, he addressed the council:

"Men of Israel, be careful what you are about to do to these men. Some time ago Theudas appeared, claiming that he was somebody great; and about 400 men joined him. But he was killed, all his followers were scattered, and his movement died out.

"After this, Judeas the Galilean appeared during the time of the census; he also drew a crowd after him, but he also was killed and all his followers were scattered.

"And so in this case now, I tell you, do not take any action against these men. Leave them alone, for if this plan and work of theirs is a man-made thing, it will disappear; but if it comes from God you cannot possibly defeat them. . . ."

The council accepted Gamaliel's argument and had the Jesus-followers whipped and released, again under an injunction "never again to speak in the name of Jesus."

Unconfirmed rumors indicate the church has gone underground, but that despite persecution and threat; its numbers continue to grow.

1 | Phenomena: The Indomitable Dream

"I want my church to grow!"

How many times have I heard this?

Roger, fifty-two years old, sat across from me at dinner. Minutes before, following an evangelism convocation, he had introduced himself to me. In an urgent voice, he had asked if we could eat together. Now we made small talk while Roger, a pastor in a Southern city, collected his thoughts.

Finally, a mist of tears welled in his eyes, as Roger leaned across the table toward me: "My church isn't growing," he said. "Yet, I want my church to grow! What's the matter with me?"

*   *   *

John, thirty-nine years old, had a ThD, a stable church of 1,500 members; he was an excellent preacher, he had a respected place among the city's ministerial community. Outwardly, he had all the symbols of success. But John didn't feel successful.

At a pastors' conference luncheon, frustration in his voice, he blurted to me: "I can't understand why my church doesn't grow. I've tried everything. What am I doing wrong? Am I placing too much emphasis on ministries that don't lead to growth . . . am I wasting my time on pointless programs?

"What can I do? Why doesn't my church grow?"

*   *   *

Ruth, thirty-four years old, began asking questions almost as soon as I began speaking. Finally, in impatience, I turned to her: "Your questions reflect a deep frustration. Can you share it with us so we can deal with the real problem—and then get on with the meeting?"

With some bitterness, Ruth said: "You Southern Baptists

have a reputation for church growth. Well, my husband pastors in another denomination and our church isn't growing.

"We don't understand why. But he is so depressed he is ready to quit the ministry. He can't seem to get his hands on why he is failing . . . . We need help.

"If he quits, I don't know what we'll do. The ministry is his calling."

*   *   *

Bill, twenty-seven years old, had just received his doctor of ministry degree. He would leave seminary in a few days to become pastor of a small church. His potential was great—but Bill was scared. "I don't know what I'm going to do," he told me the afternoon of graduation. "I've learned so much—but now I'm on my own. I'm not sure I can apply what I've read and heard. I'm afraid I might fail.

"What can I do to make sure the church grows?"

*   *   *

Paul, thirty-two years old, pastored a small, rural church. But Paul was aware of new possibilities for the church as families began moving to his Sunbelt community. After an evening service, we sat in his tiny, ill-equipped office and talked.

"Oh, there are plenty of unchurched folks around here—more every day, it seems," Paul said. "But we're not reaching them.

"Sure, we've got all the institutional programs, even missions organizations. But we're so steeped in tradition we're hog-tied. Our folks don't seem to care about the newcomers. They seem satisfied to baptize their children and keep the church one big, closed family.

"I don't know if they want just to perpetuate their own leadership, or if they just don't understand the nature of the church, but it's taking all the joy out of this pastorate.

"I don't know how I can go on if they don't believe the church should be growing."

*   *   *

Dan, forty-four years old, was among his church's most active laymen. We were standing together, awaiting his pastor, when Dan suddenly said: "You know, I enjoyed your talk tonight, but I almost didn't come.

"I tell you, these meetings are wearing me thin. It's one thing after another; sometimes five nights a week I'm driving a member of my family up here to church. And that doesn't count Sundays."

His voice evidenced resentment. "Yet I don't see the church getting anywhere. We don't seem to be growing much. I wonder if all this activity is worthwhile?"

*   *   *

Elaine, thirty-eight years old, was church secretary for a congregation of 475 in a growing suburb. For the past four years, Elaine had watched as the membership remained static, while new houses sprouted over the area.

"Our pastor's one of the hardest working men I've ever known, and one of the best," she told me one evening after a revival service.

"But I don't know how long we'll have him. He sees the possibilities for growth, but he can't seem to get the church to grow. He said the other day, 'Elaine, we've been on dead center so long I don't know if I can ever move this church. Maybe the best thing would be for me to move.'

"He's the kind of man we need," Elaine went on. "But I've wondered, is he right? Will it take new blood to get the church growing again? Why doesn't our church grow?"

For centuries, the answer to that question has intrigued pastors, religious philosophers, seminarians, church leaders, lay persons—all who believe in church growth as an ultimate expression of Christian outreach and discipleship.

"I want my church to grow."

Expressed again and again, in ways subtle and severe, this has become the plaintive cry of a generation being swamped by secularism, of a people who see their past and their future being overwhelmed by a hedonistic present.

In whatever form heard, it is the goal, the ambition, the indomitable dream, of churchpersons the world over.

While a church's statistics are on the upswing, questions of why, how, who, when are seldom asked; security insolates the church. But should the church become static, troubles follow: pastors and membership, feeling the strain, begin by doubting the direction and guidance of the church; they end by questioning the spiritual integrity and motivation of each other—and themselves.

Pastors, in our success-oriented, numerically conscious society, are especially vulnerable. As their measuring rods of progress, too often they depend on numbers in worship services, dollars in collection plates.

But counting noses or pennies is no way to judge the reality of the dream. For the indomitable dream of growing a church stretches far beyond statistics. In its depth and beauty and size, the growing church must be mirrored against the example of the New Testament congregation: "By the miracle of her own life, an exemplary community, a model of what human society should be."

Born of the Spirit, habitat and instrument of the Spirit, the early church grew rapidly: from thirty at the cross; to 120 in the upper room; to more than 3,000 on the day of Pentecost; from a lonely, provincial nation to the boundaries of civilization in 300 years.

Charging full strength on the world, with unprecedented power, believers confronted pagan people and government and religious resistance.

And their faith literally turned the world upside-down.

As they swept from Jerusalem to Rome—and beyond—they projected the varied and total ministry of their Lord: healing of the sick and lame; comforting the sorrowing; discipling the newly converted; establishing and developing churches; evangelizing the lost; and crossing all barriers—racial, economic, social—to pray, praise, worship, fellowship, evangelize, disciple, minister in the name of Jesus Christ.

Conceived of mission, nurtured as mission, empowered by the Holy Spirit indwelling in persons to be on mission, the New Testament church reached out from a base grounded in God's love as disclosed supremely in the cross. Its mandate was the Great Commission; its message was triumphant: hope, joy, love, peace, abundant life.

Both the mandate and the message are ours today.

Applying them in the confrontation and penetration of society by the church of the twentieth century stands as our responsibility.

If the church is threatened with survival, it is because it has failed to accept its mandate or proclaim its message. Gimmicks and super-energized programs do not bring renewal or rejuvenation; adaptation to secular mentality negates the church's unique role and pushes it further into the shadow of pointless, outdated organizations.

But to discover afresh the wonder and glory and power of the gospel—therein lies the church's raison d'être, therein lies the church's opportunity for sustained, honest, meaningful growth in numbers, in maturity, in ability to influence the society surrounding it.

The church wasn't created to be stagnant. Nor was the church created to be secure or insouciant. When any activity—traditional, practical, materialistic, denominational—undercuts the church's ability or willingness to risk, to push itself toward its biblical demands; growth, in its myriad forms, ceases.

The challenge of the church today is to accept the claims and promise of the gospel: Jesus is Lord of life and death; the hope of humankind. His followers are to example his life and death and gift of caring in this world. Through their actions in witnessing, discipling, and healing, they are to create an atmosphere in which church growth results.

For church growth is our Lord's intent; it is his purpose. And it must be the goal, the call, of every follower.

It must always be the indomitable dream.

"Go therefore and make disciples of all the nations, baptizing them in the name of the Father and the Son and the Holy Spirit, teaching them to observe all that I commanded you; and lo, I am with you always, even to the end of the age" (Matt. 28:19–20, NASB).

News Item 2

PHOENIX, ARIZ.—Using a theme of sharing Christ in the normal traffic patterns of life, and an attitude of never let up, Richard Jackson has led North Phoenix Baptist church in an outreach campaign that has quadrupled the church's membership in nine years.

When Jackson came to Phoenix in late 1967, the twenty-eight-year-old church had some 1,300 members. Today its membership totals more than 7,000. More than 3,500 people attend its three Sunday morning services and more than 200,000 others view its main 11 A.M. worship service on television.

In the ten years Jackson has pastored North Phoenix, he has baptized 4,500 people, 70 percent of whom are adults. He baptizes five times each week, fifty-two weeks a year.

Some 30 percent of the church's new members first heard of North Phoenix through the television ministry, estimated Walt Cavitt, church administrator.

"The others who join," Cavitt added, "are the result of personal witness. People in their everyday walks of life— whatever they're doing—they talk about the church.

The church uses more than 400 volunteers in its Monday night visitation program, but "we can't keep up with the people who visit us," Cavitt said.

"This isn't canvassing at random in neighborhoods," Cavitt added. "This is follow-up on legitimate, active leads."

North Phoenix, located in a metropolitan section near the geographic center of the Phoenix area, draws its members from all over the Phoenix area; some come from as far away as 25 miles.

"We're a city-wide church," said Cavitt. "Our growth has come because we're attracting people from all over."

It has been sustained, steady growth.

Jackson said he has never baptized more than 25 persons on a single Sunday, but seldom baptizes less than 10, either.

Sunday School growth records indicate an average increase in enrollment of 45 per month, with the low about 30 and the high about 60 new members.

"The increases," Jackson said, "come because we constantly keep before our people the need to enlist more members."

Jackson disdains gimmicks and techniques. "We've no bananas in the bunch, no famous athletes, no Miss Something-or-other, no five dollar bills under the seat," he said.

"We don't use buses except to carry people from our parking lots to the church building. And we won't do that after we complete our new building, because we'll have ample parking near the church then."

Week-long revivals have also been discontinued by Jackson. "The last one we held was in 1968, and that was a mistake," he admitted.

"Such emphases," he said, "have a tendency to be solo efforts for which people gear up twice a year and then let the rest of the year slide."

Jackson said his church's success has caused many preachers to turn to him with their church growth problems. "But," he insisted "we don't have a program. We've just tried to find God's program and get on with it."

Jackson credited North Phoenix's

growth on its willingness to follow the commands of the Great Commission, which he feels many pastors misinterpret. "Christ promised to be with us only when we do the things he said," Jackson indicated. "The moment a church becomes satisfied with those it has won and stops reaching out, growth will stop," he said.

Although he has no program, Jackson described his philosophy of outreach based on the ministry of the spoken word.

Its three parts, as Jackson defined them, are (1) the proclamation of the word in preaching and music; (2) the teaching of the word through education—the Sunday School is North Phoenix's only evangelistic organization. Everything is channeled through Sunday School; and (3) confrontation of the word in one-to-one personal witness.

Churches which apply this formula, Jackson said, do not need charismatic or dynamic leaders. Growth will result, because Christ promised it.

Yet, he emphasized, North Phoenix works hard at outreach.

"Many are being won by our people," Jackson said. "We don't have a deacon who can't lead a person to Christ—or we wouldn't have him.

"From the first," Jackson concluded, "we abolished the distinction between laity and clergy. We have a lot of ministers at North Phoenix, but no lay persons, no clergy."

2 | Purpose: Extend or Perish

The need is obvious: the human race is being lost.

"An exploding population makes it imperative that Christians face up to the fact that millions will continue to die in their sins," writes church growth specialist Paul Benjamin, "unless congregations change their ways." [1]

"For God's methodology in salvaging society," Benjamin argues, "is still bound up in the role of the congregation."

A regenerative creation of the Holy Spirit, the church is Christ's body and his redemptive arm enfolding the world. Explains missions strategist Wendell Belew: "The true church is an outpost of the kingdom of God which has been placed in a particular spot in the world to bear witness to the lordship of Jesus Christ." [2]

Although its reason for witnessing is not self-motivated, to survive in the world, the church must grow. It must be propagative. The life of the church and its hope for the future lie in its reproductive power.

Years ago, theologian William Templeton wrote: "To evangelize is so to present Christ Jesus in the power of the Holy Spirit that people should come to put their trust in God through him, to accept him as their Savior, and to serve him as their Lord in the fellowship of his church."

"Church expansion (growth)," declares missionary Melvin Hodges, "is a continuation of redemption, in the heart of God from eternity, revealed in His Son. The ministry was imparted by Christ to His disciples, energized by the Holy Spirit, and has been given to Christians today as both gift and command." [3]

The object in Christians exercising this "gift and command" is not, it should be made clear, *church growth per se;* the purpose of growth is not to perpetuate the conditions of good men and women, but to extend the kingdom of God. The church is but the vehicle upon which God carries his kingdom into the world.

Observes evangelism professor Lewis Drummond, "God is on a mission of world redemption. And his basic plan for world evangelization is the use of the instrumentality of the church." [4]

Yet thousands of churches are not growing. Bogged down in indifference and inertia, programs begat programs, not people. Structured for mediocrity, churches satisfy institutional needs. Committees rely on manuals and perpetuate past mistakes. Wandering beyond the context and foundational systems of New Testament teachings, churches struggle in parched urban deserts and barren rural plains.

"Dying urban churches are indications of an unplanned, but nevertheless real, protest by the urban disinherited," believes G. Paul Musselman. "The streams of people who pass but never enter an urban church represents a form of unconscious picketing against the church." [5]

That indictment can be expanded to include many stagnant churches, whether urban, rural, suburban. In every case, they have ceased to function as living, breathing, thriving organisms and have become stifling organizations; in every case, such churches have forgotten that they are *not* money and methods, that they *are* theologically people, not institutions.

"The real task of the church is not keeping the organizations manned," emphasizes evangelist John Havlik, "it is witness and ministry in the world. It is so easy for us to substitute organization for the living organism of the church." [6]

For Jesus, the church would be the nerve ends through which he could touch all generations. It would be the continuing expression of his humanity, of his concern for all human beings, of his relationship to them. The church would be, for all ages, the bastion of the soul, the reservoir of his authority and resources on earth.

In the church of Jesus Christ, humans shackled by their

own moral uncertainties, willful debaucheries, perverted natures, blighted desires, and gnawing weaknesses could find freedom and purpose. Beings lost amid the degeneracy of the human condition could discover the amazing grace. In the maelstrom of hopelessness, the church would represent hope; in the whirlwind of dehumanization, it would promise personhood; in the roar of divided loyalties, it would stand for God's sovereignty.

Whenever aimless and confused humanity asked the centuries-old question, "Who is man?," the church would be the answer. It would become the rainbow's end, where individuals seeking liberation would be lifted beyond the morass of earthbound human resources to the solid plain assurance discovery of divine authority.

Jesus' church would be, simply, the lighthouse to point sinful men and women to spiritual safety through a course charted in him.

It would not live to perpetuate itself, but live to spread to others in desperate need its awareness of abundant life; its eyes—and interests—would focus on Christ, not on self.

"An evangelistic outreach by the congregation which stresses a comfortable house of worship, a paved parking lot, an outstanding pulpit minister, an attractive youth program (or some similar emphasis)," points out Paul Benjamin, "is to be faulted if the underlying spiritual purpose of the congregation is overlooked . . . . A congregation which keeps pointing to itself misses the reason for its existence." [7]

Agrees John R. W. Stott, "Christ sends the church into the earth to be its salt . . . its light. The call to the church (is) to live ex-centeredly, to find its center not in itself but outside itself; to turn itself outwards to the world and to be truly a church for others." [8]

God took the initiative to reveal his love for humankind when he sent Jesus to die that all might live. God became incarnate. As a result, the church and the good news have the opportunity to declare human restoration in a new experience for each person: salvation through conversion.

This act of obedience, this change of life-style from old ways to new, is the basis of church growth. Once heard and accepted, the good news must be repeated. The world still awaits the answer to Christ's question: "Who do you say I am?" Proclaiming the answer becomes the purpose of every believer. The church becomes the motivator, the equipper, the one who sends out. The church grows when believers recognize that none are exempt from carrying out the Great Commission. As Orlando E. Costas writes in *The Church and Its Mission: A Shattering Critique from the Third World,* "Church growth is that holistic expansion which can be expected spontaneously from the everyday action of the church functioning as a redemptive community." [9]

Clearly Christ's death for our wrongs, his resurrection which offers forgiveness, his gift of life for all who repent offers absolute justification for growing and developing churches. Without this central focus, church growth concerns loose their rootage.

In brief, the good news is: God supremely disclosed his love at the cross where he broke the power of sin. The resurrection demonstrates God's power over death, man's last enemy. These constitute the divine action which decisively defeated the demonic power. This is the heart of Christianity. For that purpose God willed that none should perish.

Now God has chosen his people, the people of God in Christ, to announce to the world and to their neighbors through their experiences and their realizations that the good news is real. When God is in the heart of men, living in them, he is in position to create an atmosphere where churches grow.

In the growing church, optimism rises above pessimism: humanity, society can be redeemed. All things shall be brought under his control; not every personal desire will be satisfied, but Christ will give strength and fulfillment and the assurance of something beyond ourselves.

Christ's liberating love sweeps away hopelessness; lives are transformed. And that good news demands proclamation.

Such a realization was the wellspring of the early church. It burst forth in one of history's greatest examples of a movement's growth and flowering. Because of the presence of the Holy Spirit and the unique characteristics given the early church by Christ, the churches of the first centuries grew strong and multiplied.

They grew without grand designs or thoroughly delineated schemes. "The apostles did not sit down and map out the strategy for their world conquest," writes missionary Hodges. "Christ did not neglect the training and instruction of His disciples, but He was primarily concerned they grasp the significance of the Cross, Resurrection, and the indwelling Spirit. The apostles advanced, driven by that Spirit rather than following carefully planned tactics." [10]

Read the commission given by Christ to his disciples; read the accounts of church growth and movement in Acts. Conquests came, world views changed, because the early followers knew Jesus Christ wanted them to multiply and the seedbed for his work's growth was the local church.

New Testament local congregations became example nerve centers for all ages. A sending evangelism produced these local fellowships. They in turn made evangelism and missions their main business.

Early church members acted from deep personal conviction; in each individual experience, Christ deepened the sense of personal responsibility. Growth was spontaneous, but based on sound biblical theology, not frothy sentimentalism or emotional projects.

"Theology for action and theology in action is the standard of the New Testament," says missions professor Cal Guy. "Without redemptive involvement the very purposes of God are thwarted, and no amount of theology, however skillfully stated, can make up for that loss." [11]

Former Southern Baptist evangelism leader C. E. Autrey adds, "Theology is to evangelism (church growth) what the skeleton is to the body. Remove the skeleton and the body becomes a helpless quivering mass of jelly-like substance. By means of the skeleton the body can stand erect and move. The great systems of theological truths form the skeleton which enables our revealed religion to stand." [12]

Outreach is compulsive and unrestricted when success is measured against the yardstick of Christ's teachings. The New Testament witnesses reached out of the joy of their newfound faith; they unhesitantly presented Christ as the answer to life's basic needs.

To different people with their different references of thought, the gospel of redemption by grace through faith in Jesus had to be understood, verbalized, preached, and related to all the complexities of interpersonal relationships. To be New Testament Christians with the New Testament experiences of faith, believers must move in the same way in our world.

Church growth will result, a natural by-product of the witnessing act. Paul, the first great missionary/church starter, tore the gospel from Jewish soil and rooted it in the soil of humanity. In practicing outreach, demanded by the very content of the good news, he participated in church growth.

"No wonder Paul expended his energies so lavishly in founding and nurturing churches," Penrose St. Amant has observed. "His conception of the missionary task involved both. Evangelism for him was church-centered and the church was the seedbed of evangelism. It never occurred to Paul to travel over the Mediterranean world seeking individual converts left to their own devices or to enlist people to join this or that church as if the church were a community one joined in order to become a Christian. He thought of Christian conversion and the church as two sides of the same coin. The point is that the Pauline conception in Christ involved both individual conversion and a sharing in Christ's body, the church." [13]

The church on mission has no less responsibility. God's will is expressed through legitimate church growth: the action of people being transformed from cogs in so much machinery to a living, dynamic force of Christ and his ministry. Awareness of people—who they are, where they are, what their needs are—and a willingness to speak relevantly to them is a must for the church. To seek people just to expand the influence and power of the institution itself is the grossest sort of misuse and abuse of Christ's message; an insidious sort of blasphemy.

Concern must be genuine.

The object must not be just to grow churches, but to reconcile persons to Christ. We're not to fold our hands in the seclusion of our stained glass fortresses; to do so would be to neglect the responsibility with which we are charged. Our mission is to go; and in going, we pray, dream, work, anticipate, and trust him for results.

"We must confront men with Christ and His demands regardless of their rejection of or objection to the primary task of mission," says Cal Guy. "He (Jesus) said, 'Decide!'—we must not say, 'Discuss.' He said, 'Follow!'—we must not say, 'Compare.' . . . We must make certain that our discussion and effort lead to decision about Him. Christian mission must intend that, through every methodology, men (and women) do in fact accept Christ, become living members of His churches, and go on to win others to Him." [14]

Proclaiming the gospel with the purpose of persuading condemned and lost sinners to put their trust in God is God's will for us today. The people of each age have the right to hear the unchanging good news; announcing that message—the act of evangelism—includes every possible way of reaching outside the church to bring people to faith in Christ and membership in his church.

Never manipulative or abrasive or self-serving, always a respecter of persons, evangelism is the logical personal response to the indwelling of the Holy Spirit. As the individual is filled with joy, so he wants to give joy in return. Evangelism's effervescence causes Christians to celebrate the good news amidst people of whatever circumstance.

Evangelism goes to people; it can never be confined to Sunday pulpits only.

Myron Augsburger describes evangelism as the solicitation of persons to yield their lives to Christ and experience the regeneration of the Holy Spirit. But, he adds, its nature and conduct is "one of the tests as to whether a worshipping group is more than a mutual admiration society, an organization for devotional therapeutics, an opportunity for development of aesthetic appreciation, or a weekly class in Christian ethics." [15]

John R. W. Stott says biblical evangelism is "part of God's mission through God's church in God's world . . . . It includes the kind of dialogue in which we listen humbly and sensitively in order to understand the other person . . . . It is the offer on the ground of the work of Christ, of a salvation which is not present possession and future prospect. And it invites a total response of repentance and faith which is called conversion, the beginning of an altogether new life in Christ, in the church and in the world." [16]

Recently some members of an inner-city church in Baltimore, Maryland, were asked to define the phrase, "to evangelize." They cut through theological jargon with a simple response: To evangelize, they decided, is "to show our community we love them. It's a matter of being the love of God. It's doing, going. It's acting like Christ."

Sharing Christ is not only to proclaim the gospel to everyone and to disciple effectively the peoples of the earth, but also to bear witness to the truth of all the gospel. It implies affirming in the actions of the church the truth with regard to the work of Christ.

Christ put the church in the world to be about mission. It is to communicate his message of hope for humanity's condition. This cannot be accomplished until the church members become a sharing community—a reconciled community—excited about their potential, alive to their future. Activities and organizations cannot substitute for purpose.

For the church, in the final analysis, is nothing more than "Two or three gathered in my name"—(Matt. 18:20) and frail humans given strength and direction by the cross. Church members who sit around and talk about the business of touching the world, grow moss while the world revolves around them.

Each day, the average church member in the United States comes into direct contact with at least thirty different people. The manner in which those contacts are conducted may be our greatest clue to potential growth of the church and of Christianity itself.

Notes

[1] Paul Benjamin, *The Growing Congregation*, (Cincinnati, Ohio: Standard Publishing, 1972), p. 28.

[2] M. Wendell Belew, *Churches and How They Grow*, (Nashville: Broadman Press, 1971), pp. 19–20. Used by permission.

[3] Donald Anderson McGavran, Editor, Robert Calvin Guy, Melvin L. Hodges, and Eugene A. Nida, *Church Growth and Christian Mission*, (New York: Harper & Row Publishers, Incorporated, 1965), p. 27.

[4] Lewis A. Drummond, *Leading Your Church in Evangelism*, (Nashville: Broadman Press, 1972), p. 23. Used by permission.

[5] G. Paul Musselman, "Evangelism and the Disinherited," *Evangelism and Contemporary Issues*, edited by Gordon Pratt Baker, Copyright 1964 by Tidings. Used by permission of Discipleship Resources, P.O. Box 840, Nashville, Tennessee 37202, p. 100.

[6] John F. Havlik, *The Evangelistic Church*, (Nashville: Convention Press, 1976), p. 116. Used by permission.

[7] Benjamin, *The Growing Congregation*, p. 8.

[8] Taken from a paper presented by John R. W. Stott to the Congress on World Evangelization, Lausanne, Switzerland, 1974.

[9] Excerpted from *The Church and Its Mission: A Shattering Critique from the Third World* by Orlando Costas, Copyright 1974, by Tyndale House Publishers, Wheaton, Illinois. Used by permission.

[10] McGavran, Guy, Hodges, and Nida, *Church Growth and Christian Mission*, 27.

[11] Ibid., pp. 42–43.

[12] C. E. Autrey, *Basic Evangelism*, (Grand Rapids: Zondervan, 1954), p. 63.

[13] Penrose St. Amant, Paper on "Support of Missions in the Pauline Churches and in the Practice of Paul," delivered to Stewardship Conference, Lake Yale Baptist Assembly, Florida, 1975.

[14] McGavran, Guy, Hodges, and Nida, *Church Growth and Christian Mission*, pp. 50–51.

[15] Myron S. Augsburger, *Invitation to Discipleship*, (Scottsdale, Pennsylvania: Herald Press, 1964), p. 65.

[16] Stott.

"And I also say to you that you are Peter, and upon this rock I will build My church; and the gates of Hades shall not overpower it. I will give you the keys of the kingdom of heaven; and whatever you shall bind on earth shall have been bound in heaven, and whatever you shall loose on earth shall have been loosed in heaven" (Matt. 16:18–19, NASB).

News Item 3

NASHVILLE, TENN.—Two Rivers Baptist Church has been growing like country and western music: phenomenally.

And the excitement centered on the 3,000 member church here seems no more likely to abate than the nation's interest in the Nashville sound.

Two Rivers has coupled extensive use of media with a willingness to experiment in ministry in its fifteen-year odyssey of steady expansion.

Taking its cue from the Grand Ole' Opry and Opryland, which sit across the highway, Two Rivers has attempted to provide for tourists and homefolk alike, said pastor Jim Henry.

"Our people are willing to move with the Holy Spirit," said Henry, Two River's pastor for thirteen of its fifteen years.

"They're not locked in tradition," he continued. "They're open. They're sensitive to the Holy Spirit. They don't always say, 'We can't do it, we've never done it before.'

"They say, 'Let's do it!' "

In Sunday services ranging from a campground ministry to a drive-in church to three morning worship hours, Henry or one of his laypersons spoke to more than 3,200 people on a recent Sunday.

Another 100,000 watched Henry on television, in a broadcast that combines elements of the Sunday 11 A.M. service with a "special appeal to the television audience," Henry explained.

The special TV "invitation" results in more calls than the counselors can handle, Henry said.

In addition to television, Two Rivers church uses billboards and handbills in motels, hotels, and campgrounds to announce its services. Special events in the life of the congregation—the Easter sunrise service, the Christmas pageant, for example—are advertised in newspapers and radio spots.

Henry also reaches 50,000 people in an early morning devotional on television; letters come daily as a result of the broadcast.

Church membership surveys reveal newcomers have learned of the church through all these media.

But the church doesn't rely solely on media to increase its appeal and enlarge its membership.

"Our main factor in growth," said Henry, "is our people. They witness." Their efforts are given strength by prayer. "It's the connecting link with God," Henry said. "Our people get on their knees and pray—for each other and for lost people."

Men pray at the church each morning of the week; a women's group meets once weekly to pray "for ourselves as well as for others."

Henry has also instituted a number of programs. Among them are:

Deacon Yokefellows. Deacons pair with other laymen in a caring ministry for families: "They visit, acknowledge birthdays, go to people in the hospital—do for their families whatever they can," Henry said. The deacon-layman team also involves more people in the "caring ministry," Henry added.

Evangelism Explosion. Henry modified the evangelism outreach of the "Kennedy Plan" for his church's needs; he trained the first four volunteers a few years ago. Today more than 160 persons are trained in evangelism and the church trains another fifty per year.

Christian Life Center. When Henry started the full-scale recreation program, it was "a whole new departure for this area" because of the conservative tradition, he said. But "it has been a blessing to us. We've had additions because of it."

Teacher's Training. Before an inexperienced or untrained person becomes a Sunday School, Church Training or Bible study teacher, he or she goes through a four-month study program that includes methodology and an internship. "We're constantly turning out new, qualified teachers—not just throwing people into the classrooms," said Henry. "This has really helped us grow."

Two Rivers Church, located on a parkway that makes it within twenty minutes of "anyplace in metropolitan Nashville," Henry said, draws people from as far away as Kentucky.

But they come on their own—the church uses no buses, except one that goes to two Nashville colleges to pick up thirty-five to forty students each week.

As a result, most of the people Henry baptizes are adults—and he baptized 240 among the church's 700 additions this past year.

In the final analysis, however, Henry insisted that the church's growth "is not our doing."

"We just sit back and cry with joy at what God's doing," he said.

3 | Principles: Biblical Dynamics

For generations, church-growth specialists have honed and refined the basic concepts of church growth. Based on New Testament practices, traditional experiences, and proven methods, they revolve around the message of Jesus Christ and the commission given his disciples.

The commission is the business of disciples.

Making disciples is the business of the church.

"The two great factors influencing church growth are," writes theologian Eugene Nida, "(1) the supernatural—(i.e., the work of the Holy Spirit); and (2) the human.

"The work of God is not, however, an isolated element in church growth, but one that completely interpenetrates the basic human factors, which are primarily (a) communication; (b) economics, in the broad sense of the term; and (c) leadership . . . .

"One must constantly bear in mind that none of the factors affecting church growth can be fully understood apart from a recognition of the role of the Spirit." [1]

The Holy Spirit must permeate all the processes by which the church seeks to fulfill its mission; without the Holy Spirit's indwelling, church growth cannot occur. A church may increase in size, but unless the Holy Spirit is present, numerical growth is flimsy, like a house of cards. And the kingdom of God does not grow.

"Actually 'church growth' means all that is involved in bringing men and women who do not have a personal relationship to Jesus Christ into fellowship with Him and into responsible church membership," [2] says Fuller Seminary professor Peter Wagner.

Wagner lists some of the characteristics found in a healthy, growing church:

"Positive traits are clear; enthusiasm; obvious warmth at work in the fellowship.

"Friendliness is prevalent; flexibility rather than rigidity; high concern for the individual replaces concern for ritual." [3]

Baptist mission strategist Wendell Belew describes the church in numerous ways, including "an organism of action."

And evangelist John Havlik, calling the church "God's only institution for accomplishing world evangelization," says the church is "the body of Christ ministering to one another; the body of Christ ministering to persons out of Christ and out of the church.

"The church," Havlik concludes, "as a body reproduces itself in new members. They will reproduce themselves in new believers." [4] And the cycle will continue until Christ's return.

But how does this occur? What principles are at play in the reproductive system of church growth?

Although not every specialist agrees on every technique, most agree that, in one form or another, the following five principles are present in any church that experiences sustained, legitimate growth:

1. Biblically based concepts,
2. Bold evangelism,
3. Broad involvement of people,
4. Burning passion of the pastor,
5. Basic Faith.

Where these elements combine with the indwelling Holy Spirit, there is inevitable growth. The challenge is to bring all of the principles simultaneously to bear on the process of church growth.

The process begins with the church's reaffirmation of the New Testament as its basic source book. In it are the criteria by which church growth principles are developed and fulfilled. The examples of New Testament churches, the teachings of our Lord, the work of the apostles are clear and unquestionable.

The church, as "a spring of living water," has the responsibility of proclaiming God's grace; the church is God's instrument. But it is only as strong as its members will it to be. Jesus didn't give the church the role of his body on earth to see it sit in oblivion on remote street corners, or sanctimoniously grow by the exclusive process of inbreeding.

He intended the church to reach out, as he had, drawing to him all the elements of society: rich, poor, black, white, brown, accepted, outcast, male, female, Jew, and Gentile.

Believers who had known Jesus when he lived, became fanatical after the resurrection. They proclaimed, they taught, they made disciples, they ministered. Though threatened by the same authorities who crucified Jesus, they could not "but speak the things which we have seen and heard" (Acts 4:20).

The freshness of Christ's message burst on that historical scene with the fury of a cleansing spring rain. Paul's example further clarified the church's potential and responsibility: growth, extend yourself . . . or perish.

The people of God moved with a force that was uncontrollable. None could explain their love, their enthusiasm, their aggressive spirit, their dynamic outreach. "The early church grew," says a British scholar, "because it out-thought, out-lived, and out-died everybody around it."

If today's church growth is to match that example, it must be based on the same principles that gave the early church its impetus. Its roots must be theologically sound.*

"As an overall principle," observes pastor Calvin Miller, "there is an astounding correlation between those who hold doctrine in its conservative expression and those who win souls and consequently experience church growth." Dean Kelley, in *Why Conservative Churches Are Growing*, makes the same point.

But true church growth does not hinge on a polarized theological axis. It does hinge on a church's ability to

---

* See Appendix A for Group/Individual Study of Biblical Perspectives

evaluate and apply biblical principles. Scriptural practices overshadow all other considerations. Biblical authority is the foundation on which sound church growth theology is built.

In his preaching, teaching, and healing, Christ demonstrated the methods by which men came to know him. But even more so, in his personal contacts and relationships with those about him, he set an example for every generation of Christians. In Acts 2:47 is recorded the result of the actions of those who followed his lead: "And the Lord added to the church daily such as should be saved."

Yet church people cannot follow Christ's example of witness and ministry—if they do so without boldness.

Church growth specialist Lyle Schaller of Yokefellow Institute describes one characteristic of a dynamic, growing church as "an emphasis on evangelism . . . which is more than an attitude or rhetoric . . . . Its most important expression in lay persons who have a faith to share, a burning desire to share it, an ability to articulate that faith in witnessing to others, a firm conviction the church represents the body of Jesus Christ, a concern for people outside the church, and a willingness to help others make a response to the challenge of the Christian gospel." [5]

The whole church is to be a boldly evangelistic organism. Explains British Methodist W. E. Sangster, "Evangelism is going to the people outside. It is the proclamation of the good news of God in Jesus Christ to 'them that are without' . . . . It is the sheer mark of the Herald who goes in the name of the King to the people who, either openly or by their indifference, deny their allegiance to their rightful Lord. He blows the trumpet and demands to be heard." [6]

Bold evangelism must be biblically sound, church centered, educationally oriented, and energetically practiced. It involves the entire church, rather than relying on the pastor and/or visiting specialists. Bold evangelism can't be disguised in sugarcoated sermons or wrapped in colorful ribboned packages to be opened at a later date. Bold evangelism springs from the church as wild tigers from cages, a revolutionary message that can stand a hostile world's whips and snares.

Bold evangelism never retreats into the sanctuary of apathy or hides behind the guise of churchliness. Aggressive and infective, it ignores peer caution and charges. With it the pastor and the people are unafraid to be different. The church, rather than mirroring society, becomes its goal. The people of God become so radical, so unique, they draw society toward them, as a magnet draws metal shavings.

Urgency is evident in bold evangelism. A strident call to action can be heard in every growing church. And it is a frank, open, simple message that bold evangelism shouts: without Christ, none can have abundant life; all are condemned to the hell of existence without God.

But bold evangelism is not abrasive evangelism, not insultive evangelism, not angry evangelism. The bold witness weeps for humanity's condition; he or she poignantly wishes to help. He or she is sensitive to others, aware of others needs and hopes and desires and hurts. The bold witness acts first out of love.

The difference between bold evangelism and audacious evangelism is found in the heart, not the vocal cords, of the witness. Bold evangelism is the result of an individual's acceptance and celebration of God's gift of grace.

Joy is the hallmark of bold evangelism.

The bold witness offers not so much a new life as a new system of living, a life-style in which the vicissitudes of existence can be handled within the context of Christ's promise.

Bold evangelism seeks response: in public confession, in Christian identification. Bold evangelism wants church growth. But the bold evangelist knows those are but natural expressions of the internal change that Christ makes in the hearts of individuals.

"By their fruits ye shall know them" (Matt. 7:20), has seldom been what it should be: the barometer of congregational dedication. The early believers were firebrands, spreading the good news in temples, homes, and marketplaces. They were zealous and enthusiastic about Christ and what he was doing in their lives.

Such total involvement of church people today sounds almost revolutionary. Says English writer Michael Green, "In contrast to the present day, when Christianity is highly intellectualized and dispensed by a professional clergy to a constituency increasingly confined to the middle classes, in the early days the faith was spontaneously spread by informal evangelists, and had its greatest appeal among the working classes." [7]

Revolutionary as it may seem, the people of the church who are awakened, developed, and equipped are the most effective agents for reaching persons outside the faith. Every believer is a witness. Making the believer into the kind of witness who lovingly and aggressively tells others about Christ, is the role of the church.

A church that slumbers can hardly excite its people to involvement in ministry. A church that fears its community can hardly challenge its people to embrace the world. A church that rests sole authority on the pastor can hardly pry its members out of the spectator seats and make them participants in the action.

Yet the people of God must be actively involved in the real ministry of the church. Not everyone will have the gift of preaching or teaching; not all will be evangelists. But each member of the congregation can witness to his faith.

Perhaps the greatest challenge facing the church today is renewal and training of the laity. In too many churches the pastor has been designated surrogate priest for members too lazy, too timid, and too uncertain to do the work of witness and ministry.

The Christian army has become a force of "hired mercenaries," rather than an army conscripted by commitment to Christ. The intent of the body of Christ is that each part be a minister of reconciliation whose acts and words testify to his or her faith.

The artificial gap between the role of the priest and the lay person must be closed; church members must be freed from structure and organizational bonds so that they can do the work of the living Lord in this world.

Where programs expedite the process of witness and ministry, they are good and should be kept. But why make new structures just to fit organizational patterns if in so doing, people are drawn away from the primary task of relating to the world's agony?

A church that encourages broad involvement of its members is taking a people perspective more than a program point of view. When people have an opportunity to express their different gifts and different needs, they can commit themselves to a deeper, fuller, and richer sort of Christian service.

Jesse Bader incorporates the values of broad-based personal involvement in his criteria for growing an evangelistic church:

1. A warm evangelistic atmosphere. It is impossible to have evangelistic results in a church where there is a cold, indifferent and apathetic attitude toward the winning of others to Christ.

2. A deep concern for the lost. The same passion and concern for the lost that was in the heart of Christ must also be in the heart of the congregation.

3. The practice of prayer. "Prayer changes things" and it can and will change the evangelistic outlook and concerns of any congregation.

4. Christians, a channel of power. The Holy Spirit was given in order that Christians might ever be powerful for witnessing in behalf of Christ.[8]

Members of today's church, committed to Jesus Christ, can once again be significant instruments of God; ordinary men and women doing ordinary tasks in extraordinary ways.

Few churches, however, will have an inspired laity unless their pastors are passionate evangelists.

Today, the pastor is expected to function as prophet, administrator, comforter, evangelist. But most of all, he is the leader; he sets the pace; he makes the emphases; he guides the congregation.

Normally, the church will do no more than the pastor wishes.

Paul expressed his priority task as sharing the good news and bringing persons to Jesus Christ. The pastor who expects his church to grow will have the same outlook.

Growing churches invariably have pastors who go to the pulpit with eloquent, positive Bible-preaching sermons. The pastors practice sound Bible teaching.

Such churches not only see "incarnational witness as an essential part of her mission, but conversely it ought to liberate the proclamation of the gospel from the notion that it merely fulfills a 'spiritual' role" in the life of human-kind, believes Latin America's Costas. In them and in the outlook of their pastors, "preaching must also be seen in terms of social action because (theologically speaking) it aims at the total transformation of man." [9]

The pastor in his free and responsible pulpit speaks with authority and forcefulness. His message is the same which has uplifted generations:

His preaching is "in a ruptured society that is seeking reality," writes evangelism professor Lewis Drummond. "God's incarnation says that He cares and came to save: 'God was in Christ reconciling us (the world) to Himself (2 Cor. 15:19).'. . . .In the despair that clutches the lives of many, there is a gospel of hope. Death has been con-quered: 'He was raised on the third day . . . (1 Cor. 15:4) . . . .' This is the 'good news.' " [10]

The pastor's burning desire is that his message will sink deep into the lives of his church's members as well as into the hearts of unbelievers. But to communicate his message to the external audience, the pastor has to recognize his responsibility to influence the internal audience—those who are already "his flock." He must be "concerned about and responsible to their spiritual needs, and happy in his work as a pastor," believes Lyle Schaller. If he has these things, his burning passion will be infectious. Church members will catch that spirit and the membership will radiate outward, in warming rays of hope and love shining in a cold, dark world.

In them will come such a ground swell of active faith that church growth results as surely as flowers after spring rains. Active faith is the life-giving nucleus of church growth. It involves a physical, emotional, intellectual, spiritual commitment. It necessitates a leap beyond sensory knowledge and it grows and thrives as it is practiced.

Active faith moves mountains; active faith walks hand in hand with God. Active faith trusts.

And any church so filled with active faith will find its pastor and its membership responding with the life-giving, personal expression of Christ's gift to humankind.

Notes

[1] McGavran, Guy, Hodges, and Nida, *Church Growth and Christian Mission*, p. 175.

[2] C. Peter Wagner, *Your Church Can Grow*, (Glendale, California: Regal Books Division, G/L Publications, 1976), p. 12. Used by permission.

[3] Ibid., pp. 32–33.

[4] Havlik, *The Evangelistic Church*, p. 104.

[5] Lyle Schaller, "Seven Characteristics of Growing Churches," from *Church Administration*, October 1975 © Copyright 1975. The Sunday School Board of the Southern Baptist Convention, all rights reserved. Used by permission.

[6] W. E. Sangster, *Let Me Commend*, (Nashville: Abingdon Press, 1948), p. 14.

[7] Michael Green, *Evangelism in the Early Church*, (Grand Rapids: William B. Eerdmans Publishing Company, 1970), p. 173. Used by permission.

[8] Based on *Evangelism in a Changing America*, by Jesse M. Bader. (The Bethany Press, Copyright 1957), pp. 61–62. Used by permission.

[9] Costas, *The Church and Its Mission: A Shattering Critique in the Third World*, p. 141.

[10] From an unpublished paper, "The Nature of the Gospel," by Tom Atwood, Pastor, Paducah, Kentucky.

"Where there is no vision, the people perish: but he that keepeth the law, happy is he" (Prov. 29:18).

News Item 4

HARRAH, OKLA.—Two and a half years ago, when Rod Masteller came to pastor First Baptist Church here, he told the congregation:

"To have a great church, basically you need three factors: love, vision, and belief."

Since then, Masteller's positive approach has turned First Baptist Church around. Attendance has almost doubled—reaching 600 on occasions—and the staid, small town church is launching an ambitious plan to witness to every home in a seventy-four square-mile area.

The project, a "phase 2" of the Action Plan devised by The Sunday School Board, will require participation of almost a quarter of the congregation of middle-class, working people.

Most of the 150 lay persons needed have already volunteered.

First Baptist Church's enthusiasm for the Action Plan, Masteller said, is just one example of its excitement in reaching people scattered over its community.

Tiny Harrah, a town of only about 2,400 people, twenty miles east of Oklahoma City, is the heart of what may become "The Capital City's" newest bedroom community. Already many of the 3,500 people wrapped around Harrah on five- and ten-acre tracts, work in Oklahoma City; others commute to a nearby Air Force base. Many of the rest are ranchers and farmers.

Because of the far-flung nature of the First Baptist Church field, Masteller enlarged a bus ministry. Between 140 and 160 children are brought to the church each Sunday for a special worship service.

But Masteller has not relied solely on the Action Plan or busing to increase the church's attendance.

Shortly after he came, Masteller held a lay renewal retreat that helped create the atmosphere of love he felt essential before growth could begin.

"The church had been down; it had had problems before I came," he explained. "During the renewal weekend, people confessed their sins against each other and got right with each other. That broke down barriers."

Steve Bushey, the church's minister of youth and music, recalled the second renewal weekend, held some weeks later, was a time when the people were really solidified in their concern for outreach.

"They learned to have faith and exercise their spiritual gifts," Bushey explained. "Things really blossomed after that."

"The church holds three revivals a year, designed to be reaping revivals," Masteller said. Carefully planned, they emphasize special events each night—from a dinner to a celebrity speaker. Newspapers and a $4,000 church-owned marquee highlight the event.

"Promotion is essential," Masteller said, "because attendance doesn't just happen. We let people know we have something special going on—and we'll do anything we can come up with that isn't off-color."

Masteller said, "Every program of the church, in fact, is basically designed to accomplish one of two purposes: win the lost or mature the saved. Any program that doesn't do that, we discard. Yet it is not programs," said Masteller, "but attitudes that make a church grow.

"The basic answer to our success," said Masteller, "is that our people have begun to love each other; they're self-giving, they look over faults of others.

"It may sound trite," Masteller said, "but the big thing is love. Our people love each other and the Lord."

4 | Priorities: Impossible Is Possible

Jesus Christ, in several terse announcements, stated his purpose in coming into the world, writes evangelist John Havlik: "He came into the world to find and save persons who are lost (Luke 19:10). He came into the world to call sinners to repentance (Matt. 9:13). He came into the world to establish a new standard of righteousness (Matt. 5:17). He came into the world to minister (serve) and to die (Matt. 20:28)." [1]

Christ's mission—"that none might perish, but that all should come to repentance"—was to be carried out in his absence by those who believed in his message and his example. Banding together for succor and stamina in a hostile environment, they became churches. As the number of Christ's followers increased, churches grew and spread.

Early church members lived a desperate sort of mission. Because, as pastor Calvin Miller has written, they viewed men and women as "hopelessly lost in their sins . . . condemned creatures . . . who would perish if they did not repent," they were driven to unparalleled limits of sacrifice. The coming apocalypse, the unregenerate state of humankind, combined to cause them to risk even their lives to bring about Christ's vision of world peace and hope.

Without their actions, they believed, much of humankind would never know the abundant life of Christ. Humankind would exist forever in torment, apart from God.

The urgency with which the first Christians viewed their task should not be diminished by time. Their legacy of action, passed from generation to generation of Christians, remains as relevant to twentieth century as to first century church members.

But the methods by which today's churches plan their actions in witnessing and ministering, are influenced by the nature of their culture, their ability to respond, and their communities' needs.

The mission of the church continues unchanged. The priorities by which the church conducts its mission do change.

Determining priorities is the first task of any church that seeks to grow in response to its actions in fulfilling Christ's commission. It is also a task that involves pastor and church leadership, primarily, but also seeks the input of every church member.

For the first requirement in setting priorities is for the congregation, paced by pastoral leadership, to narrow its focus.* In thinking, teaching, and preaching, the pastor must try to instill into his people the vision Jesus had and implemented. He must involve his leadership and his people in Christ's vision as they study what God has to say about the whole world coming to know Jesus Christ. Then if their vision is strong enough they will act on it.

Vision has been described as ability empowered with supernatural faith to relate the present to the future by means of goals. Pastor Robert Schuller of Garden Grove, California, has said that vision is "the maximum utilization of the God-given power of imagination exercised in dreaming impossible ways by which a desired objective can be attained."

In Proverbs, Solomon said, "Where there is no vision, the people perish" (29:18). Hebrew scholars have interpreted these words in revealing ways. One translation is that "where there is no vision, the people 'get out of hand' "—an implication that without vision, unity cannot exist.

Another translates "perish" as "are purposeless." Activities are diluted and the people lack direction. Two

---

* See Appendix B on Framing Statement of Purpose (Mission).

other concepts are "the people 'run wild'" and "'are naked.'" The first suggests a lack of discipline, without which no group can function coherently or intelligently; the second interpretation—"are naked"—implies a people stripped of their defenses and helpless in the world.

Clearly, whatever the correct interpretation, lack of vision is a crippling condition for God's people; certainly no fruitful activity ever came to pass without the vision of individuals.

Jesus had a vision of satisfying the needs of his people; he was the shepherd who protected the harassed and helpless sheep. He had a vision of developing his church, of equipping and empowering those who followed him. He told his disciples, "But you shall receive power when the Holy Spirit has come upon you; and you shall be My witnesses both in Jerusalem, and in all Judea and Samaria, and even to the remotest part of the earth" (Acts 1:8, NASB).

His disciples identified by baptism and matured through exposure to him and his teachings, would carry his vision to the world. They would reflect his thinking, they would share his teachings, and they would proclaim that he is hope! The vision is our legacy.

No wonder Robert Schuller cried, "If your dream is from God, then you need only to exercise his miracle-working power and you can reach the seemingly unattainable goal."

Vision can become reality when the people of God are united in prayer and effort: "It isn't the much that you say you possess that shapes your character," says Alexander McClaren, "but the little that you habitually live."

Adds John Bisagno of First Baptist Church, Houston, Texas, "Vision always hopes for something better, always expects it, always believes it will happen. The thing that makes a difference is expectancy." [2]

This is faith—believing that the impossible is possible. Church growth requires such faith. In these days of inflation, talk is cheaper than ever and growth won't come to those who say they believe, but do not act on their belief.

Growth demands work. It also demands patience with God, and with each other and belief in the ability to grow, despite circumstance, location, and difficulty. Growth deserves what Pastor Schuller calls "possibility thinking." Everything can't be done at once, yet something can be done. Today.

But what? This is the reason for determining priorities and goals, for long-range planning as well as immediate action.

The priorities of a church can be as diverse as building a gymnasium for members to conduct a coffeehouse for aimless juveniles, as eclectic as a new chandelier in a skid row mission. Priorities are set by the church's recognition of the demands of the surrounding neighborhood. Priorities are outgrowths of the church's task of witnessing and sharing, caring and healing.

New facilities and structures for organizational programs may be important, but they should always be considered in light of the questions, "Why does the church exist? What does God want of his church? How best can the church's mission be accomplished with current resources?"

From the standpoint of church growth and evangelistic outreach, God wants lost persons found, and he wants to reconcile men and women to himself through his Son, Jesus Christ.

Every other function of the church, from building to ministering to discipling, results from commission of that objective: the only way for a church to grow, to minister, to extend Christ's influence to secular society, is by the conversion of sinners to the Lord.

But, warns Myron Augsburger, "The modern church may be concentrating more attention and devotion upon the structure of the church than upon the Savior Himself. Although the church is the witness of Christ in the world, the conscience to society, the fellowship of forgiven sinners, it is only Christ who is Redeemer, the Head of the church and the Savior of the world." [3]

For the congregation struggling to come to grips with its priorities, evangelist Leighton Ford stresses, "If our goal is the penetration of the whole world, then for the agents to carry out the task we must aim at nothing less than the mobilization of the whole church." [4]

No church will grow if its members do not want growth. "If it (the church) is a growing church, it (is because it) wants to grow," says Peter Wagner of Fuller Theological Seminary. "Wanting to grow and planning for growth is another way of applying faith (principles)." [5]

Growing a church is not, however, simply pushing some pet project. Nor is it the numerical inclusion of members transferred from other churches; in such cases, an individual church might grow, but the "universal church"—the kingdom of God on earth, does not.

Writes one theologian: "Far too often the growth activities of the church simply are a stirring over again of the same people. Instead of being fishers of men, we are keepers of the aquarium and flatter ourselves when we have stolen fish from someone else's bowl."

Real, sustained church growth comes only through the conversion and baptism of those who accept Jesus Christ as personal Savior and Lord.

Such growth is thoroughly biblical, centered in Christ and supported by the Scriptures. Emphasis on numbers becomes important, therefore, only when it represents meaningful changes occurring in the lives of individuals.

In short, true church growth is the result of church people being unwilling to continue business as usual. Church growth translates into the people of God striking out to be the church of God in a pagan world.

This sort of action does not come from a program, but a process of constant rededication to the New Testament life-style. This sort of growth does not result from committees, but from a lifetime commitment to the mission of the church's existence.

"Too frequently," cautions Myron Augsburger, "the church has either been of the world and lost its witness by compromise, or it has withdrawn to avoid being of the world and thereby failed to be in the world with a creative witness." [6]

That ever-present dilemma threatens to impale many churches today. Someone has said that the church's identity comes from Jesus Christ, but its personality is dictated by the needs of the community surrounding it. Yet too often, physical, mechanical, or other institutional demands capture the church's attention and resources: the true mission of the church is lost in the constant effort to stoke the engines just to keep the organizations running.

In his book, *Your Church Can Grow,* church growth theorist Peter Wagner lists seven vital signs for church growth: (1) A pastor who is a possibility thinker and whose dynamic leadership has been used to challenge the entire church into action, (2) A well-mobilized society which has discovered, developed, and is using all the spiritual gifts for growth, (3) A church big enough to provide the range of services that meet the needs and expectations of its members, (4) The proper balance of the dynamic relationship between celebration, congregation, and cell, (5) A membership drawn primarily from one homogeneous unit, (6) Evangelistic methods that have been proved to make disciples, and (7) Priorities that are arranged in biblical order.

Priorities cannot be arranged, however, until they are defined. This requires a thorough study of the congregation and the community. What are internal resources? What are external needs? How can the churched population reach the unchurched?*

---

* See Appendix C for Self Study Guide for Church and Community, also see Appendix D for Church Member Analysis and Profile.

The church's "universes"—those target groups that make up its potential audience—should be pinpointed, and programs, activities, and outreach directed to them specifically.

For example, any community with large numbers of elderly people should have emphases designed especially for that age group. To neglect them would be to avoid an area of possible ministry and growth. Says church strategist Lyle Schaller, churches most effective in reaching people "focus on narrowly defined population groups," rather than on a single age group. A growing church will love, will go, will serve in accordance with needs.

Priorities may be defined, but they do not become active goals until they are coupled with resources and given measurable, obtainable objectives. A priority of the church may be to minister to the elderly. The objective for the next calendar year may be to set aside X amount of dollars and enlist and train X number of people for this ministry. The goal may be to involve fifty elderly people in the ministry and bring at least half of them to a saving knowledge of Jesus Christ.

The second step in drawing up the church growth blueprint, therefore, is determining resources.

The first resource is people. Discovering and applying people resources is done against the backdrop of teaching, preaching, and equipping. God gives different abilities and talents. Using the laity's potential in creative ways to accomplish church growth priorities is one of the church's greatest challenges.

Perhaps the most important task of church growth, therefore, is the initial one of energizing—renewing—the laity. To create in the congregation's human resource pool an awareness of, and possible outlet for, the gifts God has given, is vital to the life of the church itself.

Itemizing current projects and financial resources is a second step in making church growth plans. But a limitation in financial resources should not be the death knell of needed witness/ministry actions. The history of the church is replete with examples of congregations that have reached out despite monetary handicaps.

Imaginative pastors and church leaders will be able to find the resources to care for specific, legitimate needs.

Finally, inventory of material and equipment resources should be taken. Outside resources, such as equipment used by church members in their vocations or hobbies, could add significantly to the list of things a church can do.

With priorities determined and resources counted, the church should set goals.* Goals are "statements of behavior desired for a specific time," actions "the church plans to accomplish for whom, to what extent and when." Says Edward Dayton, church growth specialist, "Every goal is a statement of faith."

"The goal of any program of evangelism is to produce disciples," says Engel and Norton in *What's Gone Wrong with the Harvest*. But that goal statement is so broad, they point out, it is practically useless as a guide to church growth. They continued, "if disciples, therefore, are being produced, the outward manifestation will be measurable numerical growth within the Church. Making disciples is defined in terms of the numbers of those who accept Christ, show evidence of regeneration, and are incorporated into the Body of Christ." [7]

Goals must be measurable. They must have specific time limits; there must be quantitative and qualitative yardsticks by which to gauge their accomplishment.

Goals must also be manageable; they must be relevant; they must be personal and they must be significant— challenging. Manageable goals are reasonable and within the scope of resources. Relevant goals relate not only to need, but also to situation and environment. Goals become personal when they are incorporated by individuals. The

---

* See Appendix E for Example Worksheet for Setting Goals.

church's goals are the goals of persons and unless church members accept church goals as their own, likelihood of accomplishment is diminished.

Significant goals progress toward faith possibility. They challenge by aiming high; but they do not frustrate by aiming beyond reach. And their accomplishment will make a provable—verifiable difference in conditions and/or lives of people involved.

Setting goals means planning through combining priorities with resources. For Christians, goals also require faith that God is at work in this world. Only with that assurance can Christians set goals that are manageable, measurable, and meaningful.

Plans are the ways goals are accomplished. If the goal is church growth, an action plan is needed for church growth does not occur like spontaneous combustion. Church administration specialist Reginald McDonough suggests that serious planning assists the church in fulfilling its purpose. Churches, to be effective despite the changes of time and personnel, should learn to:

1. Act rather than react,
2. Anticipate problems and work out solutions before the problems occur,
3. Make things happen rather than let things happen,
4. Make use of circumstances rather than fret about misfortunes,
5. Listen to God speak about what the church should be and do.[8]

The Church Administration Department of the Sunday School Board suggests important benefits to the church willing to engage in creative, flexible planning:

1. *A sense of purpose.* The church will know where it is going and what it should do.

2. *A relevancy to life.* Real community needs will be examined and the most crucial ones selected for church action.

3. *A unity of concern.* Members will begin to work as one

for highly important church goals.

4. *Increased motivation.* Members will work more diligently toward the goals they helped set.

5. *Good stewardship of resources.* The church will be able to invest its resources of persons, time, money, and facilities into the areas of greatest importance to the mission of the church.

6. *A means of continuing growth.* The church will be able to perpetuate itself by facing the future and preparing to meet it.[9]

Plans turn goals into action. Plans list person or persons responsible for accomplishing goals. Plans include dates when actions should be completed. Plans take into account existing programs of the church, either to use or change so they are made responsive to goals.

Well-drawn, carefully researched plans free the church from routine and traditional methodology. Writes Engel and Norton: "A Spirit-led planning process begins, proceeds, and ends with a seeking of the mind of the Lord. This almost goes without saying, but God also expects man to do his part—'We should make plans, counting on God to direct us' (Prov. 16:9, *The Living Bible*). Man uses three bases for planning, all of which are guided and enriched by the (Holy) Spirit: (1) experience, (2) intuition, and (3) research. All three really are necessary, but all to frequently research is considered to be irrelevant."[10]

This system of determining priorities, evaluating resources, setting goals, and charting action plans could be called "church management by results."

Church growth advocates have rightfully stressed the importance of numerical, measurable goals. Numbers added to church rolls, of course, are not difficult to measure. The results of proclamation and cultivation present, however, some measurement problems.

Because not every church action or church strategy obviously can be evaluated by statistical measurement, extent of evaluation depends on the complexity of the goal and the action plans involved in carrying it out.

If, for example, the goal involves a certain event happening at a certain time, the result is clearly measurable: did it occur when planned? If, on the other hand, the goal was lay renewal, how does the church measure "deeper personal commitment"?

Evaluation criteria aren't always simple. Basically, however, they include:

1. Determine the goal to be accomplished,

2. Translate the goal into measurable indicators of achievement,

3. Collect data,

4. Compare the collected data with the indicators of achievement stated in the goal.

All goals should be evaluated. Goals that were not achieved should provide much information that can be used in the goal-setting process in the future. Were the goals unrealistic? Did they fail to capture the imagination and energy of the people? Were they not valid? Were they designed to keep the aquarium or to net new fishes? Why did they result in this manner?

By continually measuring, evaluating, and planning, the progress and process of church growth will bear results. Successes can be duplicated, failures discarded.

Accepting priorities, developing vision, identifying needs and resources, and working through goals will bring results and show the world, as well as ourselves, *the church is growing.*

Notes

[1] Havlik, *The Evangelistic Church,* pp. 27–28.

[2] John Bisagno, *How to Build An Evangelistic Church,* (Nashville: Broadman Press, 1971), p. 13. Used by permission.

[3] Augsburger, *Invitation to Discipleship,* pp. 60–61.

[4] Leighton Ford, *The Christian Persuader,* (New York: Harper and Row, 1966), p. 45.

[5] Wagner, *Your Church Can Grow,* p. 47.

[6] Augsburger, *Invitation to Discipleship,* p. 10.

[7] James F. Engel and H. Wilbert Norton, *What's Gone Wrong with the Harvest,* (Grand Rapids: Zondervan, Copyright 1975), p. 56. Used by permission.

[8] Reginald McDonough, *Leading Your Church in Long Range Planning,* (Nashville: Convention Press, 1975), p. 5. Used by permission.

[9] Ibid., p. 7.

[10] Engel and Norton, *What's Gone Wrong with the Harvest,* p. 57.

"I solemnly charge you in the presence of God and of Christ Jesus, who is to judge the living and the dead, and by His appearing and His kingdom: preach the word; be ready in season and out of season; reprove, rebuke, exhort, with great patience and instruction. For the time will come when they will not endure sound doctrine; but wanting to have their ears tickled, they will accumulate for themselves teachers in accordance to their own desires; and will turn away their ears from the truth, and will turn aside to myths. But you, be sober in all things, endure hardship, do the work of an evangelist, fulfill your ministry" (2 Tim. 4:1–5, NASB).

News Item 5

OMAHA, NEB.—In the decade since its founding, Westside Baptist Church here has grown from a few families meeting in a home prayer/Bible fellowship to 650 people attending three Sunday morning worship services.

"The keys to our growth," said pastor Calvin Miller recently, "are carefully planned and well-prepared worship experiences and dynamic evangelism."

Convinced that no evangelism program will be effective if the worship doesn't hold those who come, Miller broke with traditional patterns to institute dramas and "a festival appeal" in some services.

Order of the service changes from week to week—for the sake of change. Miller also observes most events on the Christian calendar, from Advent to Palm Sunday, a practice not common among Southern Baptists.

"Sameness gets built-in," Miller said. "We keep them on their toes. Our people seem to like it."

If Westside has been "ingenious in conserving those who join," it has also been active in enlisting new members.

The church, in a heavily Roman Catholic, upper-middle-class suburb, has averaged more than seventy-five new members annually. But its greatest increase has come in the past few years, Miller noted, after he adapted the "Kennedy Program" for his congregation.

The program, based on an approach to "personal evangelism" developed by a Presbyterian pastor, involves extensive training of lay persons in soul-winning. Miller explained, "Techniques used are not canned. They don't emphasize handing out tracts. They stress personal contact and sharing one's faith naturally."

Miller admitted his church's approaches should not be applied to churches in other situations: "I doubt I could work in a lower-class section," he said, "because my ministry and my efforts have been geared to this community."

Westside's community is one in which "evangelical Christianity is very fearful," Miller said, because it is not understood. Early efforts by the church to reach non-Christians were difficult. But as the church grew, so did the openness and acceptance of people in the neighborhood.

In 1976, for example, Westside baptized almost 100 people, accepted into membership another sixty, most of whom came on statement of faith. Few of these, Miller added, were of Southern Baptist background.

"Ninety-nine percent of the people who join our church already have been led to Christ by a member of our evangelism teams or by myself," Miller said.

He has not focused on mass evangelism efforts because he found they "lead to spurious decisions that don't result in church growth." Westside Church also abandoned a bus ministry when Miller discovered its continuation threatened the church's attempt "to be true to whom the Lord said we should be." And Miller added that being true to itself may be most important in a church's ability to grow.

Without compromising Christian principles, Miller said, "We've tried very hard to take shape from recognition of community needs. Perhaps our growth has come because we've succeeded in that," Miller concluded.

5 | Pastor: The Pacesetter

The most influential voice in the life of the church comes from the pulpit. Several times each week, the pastor has an opportunity to share his vision of the church and its mission. If he speaks with God-given assurance and urgency, the pastor can, through his weekly sermons, motivate, encourage, challenge, inspire, and infect his people with his insights into the good news.

As the acknowledged leader of most churches, the pastor can profoundly shape the ministry of his congregation. In normal situations, the church assumes the pastor's basic attributes and attitudes. If he stresses growth, growth occurs.

In a survey taken of fifteen fast-growing churches, the key factor in numerical increase in eleven of the churches was the pastor; in nine of the churches, new pastoral leadership had meant a sudden spurt in growth.

"The place of the pastor in the evangelism (growth) of the local church is strategic," says C. E. Autrey, Southern Baptist evangelism leader. "If he is evangelistic, the church will ordinarily be evangelistic. The degree to which the pastor is evangelistic will be reflected in the church. If he is lukewarm, the church will very likely be lukewarm. If he is intensely evangelistic, the church will reflect the warmth and concern of the pastor." [1]

Every pastor is inundated with demands on his time, his efforts, his energies. One pastor has remarked he felt like "the skeleton key" that unlocked all the church's programs and activities. But of all the duties of the church—from giving comfort to the afflicted to afflicting the comfortable—none has the immediacy of evangelism.

The responsibility of the pastor then is to sift through all the pressures and results and enunciate the church's priorities. And if evangelism is not high among them, the church will not grow. More important, the kingdom of God will not be realized on earth.

Many pastors single out evangelism as the church's most strategic function. They recognize, as Faris Daniel Whitesell has said, "the Pastor-evangelist, then, is the keyman in local church evangelism (growth), and local church evangelism is the key to all other evangelism." [2]

Yet other pastors emphasize other church-given tasks. They understand their mission to be the creation of a caring fellowship within; but their efforts often result in an internalized, "clubby" viewpoint that never reaches outside to replenish a membership continually decreasing through death, moving, or lack of interest.

Others preach or teach, call on the ill, comfort the bereaved, edit the church paper, and go about community public ecumenical movements. But they never find time to puncture the "web of fellowship" and seek those outside who are lost, alone, and without the knowledge of Christ's gift. And incredibly they never make this a goal of the church or lead the congregation to evangelistic outreach.

Pastor and congregation should walk in a horizontal relationship. But the effective, evangelistic pastor will walk in front. His practices will reflect his beliefs, his emphases will mirror his ideals. He will be the catalyst, through study and prayer, opening his church to the indomitable dream of church growth, his will be the equipping, the empowering role.

As he follows Christ's example, he will set the tone for the entire congregation. Evangelism professor Lewis Drummond describes the pattern set by Jesus:

"(1) Jesus unreservedly gave of himself; he shared his own personhood on behalf of the needy.

"(2) He confronted people with the great issues.

"(3) He never compromised the demanding claims of the gospel to win followers.

"(4) He had profound respect for human personality.

"(5) He presented the truth uncompromisingly and

challenged men (persons) to decide then and there.
"(6) He had a definite strategy (evidenced by his life).
"(7) He did not attempt to do all the work himself.
"(8) He was above all compassionate.
"(9) He ministered to the whole man (person).
"(10) He saw prayer as the one indispensable exercise in
his mission." [3]

When the pastor fulfills those criteria, even in his limited human way, he will express a life of credibility that will allow him to inspire and motivate his congregation. His sermons will not represent a shallow or one-dimensional gospel, but will become opportunities to sow the seeds of a Christ-like evangelism. Because it is grounded in a life practice of Christ-directed outreach, his evangelistic preaching, his church growth preaching, his mission-minded preaching will touch his congregation, shape its members' minds, and mold their thinking.

Such sermons extend far beyond the traditional "hellfire and brimstone" to instill in members a recognition of the demands of the gospel, their gift of God's grace, and their need to share what they have with others. An evangelistic preacher speaks not only to the needs of the small percentage of his audience who are lost, but also to the 95 percent of his audience who are saved—but who need the Sunday renewal experience to enter the Monday world of work with a courageous, evangelistic voice.

Feeding the congregation with truth, seeking with compassion those who stray, defending against the satanic onslaught, the pastor endeavors through his preaching and love, to equip the church for its work of ministry and mission.

This kind of preaching "expects mighty works to happen," says James S. Stewart. If the pastor realizes, adds Stewart, "that although the congregation may be small, every soul is infinitely precious. . . . Then preaching, which might otherwise be a dead formality and a barren routine, an implicit denial of its own high claim, will become a power and a passion; and the note of strong, decisive reality, like a trumpet, will awaken the souls of men." [4]

As in every church effort, the task can be overwhelming, however, if the pastor does not have vision. The importance of pastoral foresight cannot be overemphasized, therefore. Great religious leaders, from Jeremiah to Jesus, have had vision. They have been able to extract the essence of the future from the promise of the present. They have seen the hope of the world lifted above the despair of everyday life. Everyone recognizes the importance of vision. But where does vision end and recklessness begin? Where does boldness stop and audaciousness start?

Only each pastor, working in his individual circumstance, and church, depending on its individual resources, can answer those questions. For Jesus Christ, the vision of a mighty army growing from a few hesitant followers was a realistic and clear vision.

For a local pastor and congregation, burning with the same passion that Jesus possessed, the vision might be a church of two or three or five or ten times its present size. It might be a whole block or whole community or whole city rejuvenated by Christ's message.

If the pastor doesn't have the vision of church growth possibilities, the congregation probably won't. A reporter once asked missionary Glenn Igleheart if the huge numbers of lost people in New York City, where Igleheart worked, didn't discourage and overwhelm him. Igleheart replied, "No. This place offers the greatest opportunity I can imagine. Overwhelmed-discouraged? No! This is a fantastic challenge!"

Igleheart's ability to wrest hope from the jaws of defeatism needs to be duplicated in every pastor. A situation that would frighten one pastor out of his senses, challenges the pastor with vision.

God's intent for the church is the biblical perspective upon which vision is based. A church awash in "uncertain sounds" of a doubting pastor will not have the positive and definitive vision that gives it the necessary strength and assurance to penetrate the world. A church bewildered by a pastor without vision will be unable to grasp the potential and purpose for which God has created it.

But as the pastor clarifies his vision, grounding it in clearly enunciated goals and well-defined strategy, the church will come alive. Wrapped up in the learning experience, the sharing experience, the praying experience of a vision jointly held, the pastor and congregation will move forward united. The pastor who knows what God wants and the church which moves to fulfill God's purpose will be blessed. And growth will follow, as surely as oak trees come from acorns.

But vision alone is not enough. Vision demands commitment. The pastor's vision must be reflected in his thinking, his teaching, his preaching, in all his actions.

Without conviction there is loss of commitment, confusion of mission, and lack of communication.

A vision of church growth, a commitment to church growth, involves certain costs, if it is to reproduce the New Testament pattern in concept and principles. For the pastor,

• Every action must be spiritually based. The power of the Holy Spirit is available only when the church acts within the framework of our Lord's commands.

• Every action must be based on intellectually sound ideas. Half-baked plans and frivolous thinking can ruin church growth efforts. Biblical guidelines provide the foundation; awareness of the world's needs and mind-set can provide insight into appropriate methodology for local church growth.

• Every action must be an emotional outlet. Emotional concerns and emotional processes are as important as intellectual ones. An unfeeling pastor cannot generate compassion and caring in his congregation. Nor can a pastor who allows his emotions to control him, function as leader for a church. His emotional instability will soon affect his whole body—and the whole body of the church.

• Every action must be considered against physical ability. Commitment to church growth is physically demanding. The pastor who is "out front" must work twice as hard, twice as long, twice as diligently as his congregation. He does not expect his people to expend more physical energy than he is willing to give himself.*

With such vision and such conviction, the pastor can initiate church growth for his congregation. But he cannot do the task alone. A pastor who recognizes the need for true, sustained church growth must avoid the "cult of personality" by recognizing the potential of the laity.

Unfortunately, many pastors are threatened by their lay people. Rather than serve as catalyst, equipper, liberator of the laity for ministry and mission, the pastor attempts to control the lay people's expressions of their faith.

Dangerous conflicts concerning who runs the church erupt, destroying the pastor's ability to lead, the people's ability freely to reproduce themselves. Says evangelist-theologian John Havlik, "Churches reproduce churches and believers reproduce believers . . . . There can be no reproduction of churches, however, that is significant unless there is first the basic reproduction of believers within the body. No church can really be alive to its full potential in a New Testament sense that is satisfied only with additions by church letter and baptizing their children." [5]

To develop a growing church, the pastor must encourage lay participation in all the church's processes and decision-making. Genuine responsibility must be given the laity.

Motivation through preaching is useless without training through teaching; the pastor must work alongside—and yet through—the lay persons in his church, or he will never fulfill the intent of his own ministry.

---

* See Appendix F for Pastor's Personal Commitment

Crisis may occur as the lay people are given more and more opportunity. But the pastor who remembers his first responsibility is to God will sail over the rough waters into placid harbors. With courage, faith, and humility, he will act "to do, then to teach" as Christ examples. For today's pastor, faced with growing numbers of unreached people, may find his greatest potential in discovering, developing, and sending forth lay persons with their God-given spiritual gifts.

That was the pattern of church growth in the first century, it must be our pattern of church growth today.

Notes

[1] Autrey, *Basic Evangelism*, p. 63.

[2] Faris Daniel Whitesell, *Basic New Testament Evangelism*, (Grand Rapids: Zondervan, Copyright 1949), p. 133. Used by permission.

[3] Drummond, *Leading Your Church in Evangelism*, p. 55.

[4] James S. Stewart, *Heralds of God*, (Grand Rapids: Reprinted by Baker Book House, 1972, and used by permission), pp. 47–48.

[5] Havlik, *The Evangelistic Church*, pp. 103–104.

"For just as we have many members in one body and all the members do not have the same function, so we, who are many, are one body in Christ, and individually members one of another. And since we have gifts that differ according to the grace given to us, let each exercise them accordingly: if prophecy, according to the proportion of his faith; if service, in his serving; or he who teaches, in his teachings; or he who exhorts, in his exhortation; he who gives, with liberality; he who leads, with diligence; he who shows mercy, with cheerfulness" (Rom. 12:4–8, NASB).

News Item 6

JACKSONVILLE, FLA.—Parkwood Baptist Church has built a pattern of sustained, steady growth on recognizing community needs and seeking to minister to them.

Under pastor Don Everson, who came to Parkwood seventeen years ago while the church was still a mission, the church has grown to 2,350 members.

But it has matured even more as its members have sought to make loving a way of life. They work with prisoners, mentally retarded children, low-income persons, international seamen, people in nursing homes, and dozens of others often outside the reach of traditional church programs.

Parkwood sits in the Arlington area of this north Florida seaport, only an expressway divides its middle to upper-middle-class neighborhood from a low-income housing section. Nothing, however, has separated Parkwood from people, no matter what their income or background. "Our church has been very open, very accepting," said Everson.

The church's wide-ranging ministries have started simply. "We lay out a need to our people. If it strikes fire, our people pick it up. We undergird them as they need it. But, we don't pump them up and we don't beg them to stay with it.

"If they feel a ministry is not meeting a need or they lose interest, they're free to drop any program," Everson said. "But we haven't had any to drop yet," he added.

Perhaps most extensive has been the prison ministry, a "total concern" program that not only witnesses one-to-one to dozens of prisoners in three Jacksonville area institutions, including the state maximum security unit, but also works with the children and spouses and relatives of inmates. Parkwood's volunteers help prisoners get jobs while offering them opportunities for Bible study.

Few of these have become members of Parkwood, Everson admitted. Yet the program has had phenomenal results. In three years, some 1,300 prisoners have made professions of faith in Christ.

Many from the Jacksonville area did join Parkwood. "But most are not from Jacksonville, they returned home and affiliated with churches there," Everson added.

Another active ministry that has done immeasurable good, although its numerical results have not been large, is Parkwood's twenty-four-hour "prayer line."

Manned by church volunteers from 6 A.M. to 11 P.M., it offers an outlet for persons who want someone to share with or someone to pray for them. (A recording takes calls during other hours.)

Everson, who handles a line each week for an hour, said he gets from one to seven calls during this shift. "Few of those who call are added to the church's rolls," Everson said, "but some do respond to our concern and visit."

Day-camping in a low-income housing area has led Parkwood into homes with great needs. A manager of one apartment complex told Everson that the church's program has cut crime in his area by 50 percent. The manager and some families affiliated with Parkwood as a result of the ministry.

Parkwood also sponsors a day-care program for mentally retarded preschoolers, with special Sunday activities concluding the week's efforts. The ministry extends to parents and siblings of the mentally retarded children.

In addition, the church helps in a seaman's ministry in the port of Jacksonville, works with persons in the growing Filipino community, sponsors a mission in a wealthy suburb, has services and projects in a nursing home, and performs a "puppet ministry" of witness in the prison, shopping centers, and other gathering places.

Everson said that much of the church's concern grew from its experiences in lay renewal activities. "As people got a grasp of what their gifts were, they moved naturally into ministry," Everson said.

Everson has not neglected evangelism per se, with programs of witness training and discipling, such as "Witness Involvement Now" (WIN) schools.

"But," he said, "the basic point of our ministries is to touch people's needs and love them. Success or failure of our ministries isn't based on numbers.

"The real dynamic created by ministry is that it results in evangelism," Everson noted. "When loving becomes a way of life, people become evangelistic.

"The deeper-life emphases of renewal," Everson has found, "are good things when tied with outreach. When we minister we also win persons to Christ, because ministry creates a warmth to which people are drawn."

Yet for Everson and the members of Parkwood, evangelism without ministry is half a loaf. "If you screw yourself down to just visiting and preaching, you may have more additions," he commented. "But I'm not sure you're really fulfilling the Great Commission as well."

6 | People: Making Spectators Participators

Christianity was never intended to be a spectator sport. Christians are called to active participation in the world; discipleship has always demanded involvement, dedication, total commitment to the mission and ministry of our Lord.

Yet in this day of the professional clergy and staff, the Christian movement is threatened as never before. For the specialists are assuming roles within the church that never were planned for them alone, the work of evangelistic growth is being left to the pastor, the work of visitation to the sick and lost is being left to the outreach minister, the work of concern for the weak and the poor is being left to the social ministries expert.

And the Christian movement, historically a lay advance propelled by the intense desire of its adherents, is grinding to an inexorable halt after centuries of full-steam-ahead charges.

The truth is: the professional church staff alone can no more win the battle for God than a commanding general can defeat the enemy when his troops are sitting on the sidelines, with their hands in their pockets, and their minds on the chow line.

Of course, lay persons are involved in the machinery that keeps the church's organizations and structures running. They serve as Sunday School teachers and organizational clerks, as missions secretaries and committee chairpersons.

But the involvement needed today is outside the general processes related to perpetuating present church life. Outside our formal activities within the church, how many opportunities are made for contact with the unchurched? And why are so few contacts made by Christians considered chances for witness and ministry?

Not only do most Christians shun the bum on the street, a person in obvious need of God's grace; but they also sidestep possible witness opportunities in their offices, their clubs, their playgrounds, their social functions.

When the major Christian-oriented action of a church member is to help sustain the organizations and programs—no matter how good they may be—he or she is missing the most exhilarating experience of discipleship which is telling others of the significance of the cross.

Clearly the duty of the Christian today is not to sputter and hesitate, but to act. Edmond W. Robb said in a 1965 issue of *Christianity Today,* "The world does not need a better philosophy, it needs a Savior. It does not need reformation, it needs regeneration in Christ. Too often the church offers humanistic philosophy to sinners; this is giving stones when men ask for bread. We have preached morality and have not offered forgiveness and grace."

Forgiveness and grace are best expressed in the verbal and physical conduct of individual Christians; the New Testament church is the supreme example.

New Testament Christians knew every believer was responsible for carrying forward the Great Commission. Evangelism—in its broadest gospel definition—was the vocation of every follower, whatever secular avocation he or she chose to earn a living.

The early Christians' conduct and spirit impressed all about them; their compassion and love were symbols that God was at work in the world. Whether in physical or financial jeopardy, whether imprisoned or harassed, they accepted the demands of discipleship.

And, as a result of "people participation," the early church prospered and thrived.

Today's churches can seldom boast such active involvement of their lay persons. Like Ezekiel's valley of dry bones, they are lifeless. Their lay people are unstimulated by either the challenge or the opportunity of Jesus' cry, "Freely you have received, freely give" (Matt. 10:8).

In *Pentecost and Missions,* Harry R. Boer writes, "Church-growth is a command which has been given because the church has the power to obey it, because the spirit has been given to the church, and because it is here essence and natured to be a witnessing body."

The people of God are the world's salt, yeast, light. They are the kindling by which Christ's message can set the world aflame. But they cannot accept their Christian functions in the world if they are protected from the world by a shield of steeple and stained glass.

Newly converted believers have a passion and a concern for sharing their new faith. Loss of this feeling is a tragedy of the church. When it occurs, no wonder the church doesn't grow!

The reality of one's conversion initiates a new life of Christian fellowship and growth into Christian maturity; membership in the church and Christ-like involvement in the world follow. Heartbeat caring is central to the people of God because the love of Christ leaves no choice.

Our action-oriented society will not respond to a shallow word-message. Our words must live in our deeds before they are credible. A church eager to grow must also be a church eager to serve. The call is limited to those with compassionate hearts, the inconsistent and insincere need not apply.

Christ involved himself in total ministry, but he did not attempt to do the work alone. He taught and he equipped his followers so they could become the new messengers of his love and grace.

How can the unknowing find the truth of Christ's joyous promise if Christians exhibit lives of prune-like retreat? How can they understand the hope of Christ's sacrificial death if Christians live hollow, demeaning existences? How can they realize the concern of Christ's compassionate life if Christians ignore the hurts and hungers in the lives about them?

The only way for non-Christians today to witness Christ

is through the lives of his followers. People will not swap their secular life-style for a method of living that is seemingly unfruitful, negative, and uncaring.

The kingdom will not grow—individual churches will not grow—until Christians, filled with the Holy Spirit, present to the world—and to their neighbors—the true image of Jesus' death, life, and eternal love.

Explains Elton Trueblood, Quaker philosopher, "The Sunday morning worship service in every church in the land ought to be an occasion, not when we achieve simple peace of mind, but when we come together to get our marching orders for the week. Here must be a body of believers which is seen as a fellowship of conscientiously inadequate persons who gathered because they are weak, and scatter to serve because their unity with one another and with Christ has made them bold. This is the only kind of Christianity that can stand up to the challenge of the militant paganism and fanaticism of the New Left (anything unChristian)." [1]

Such a commitment on the part of lay persons creates a broad base of involvement in the local church, this is the key to church growth. For broad involvement of the people . . .

* means everyone living unapologetically to example Christ. This is no life-task of drudgery, but a reflection of the church as Christ's body on earth. Joy is apparent and experienced.

* carries the church beyond the building's walls. As lay persons discover and rediscover their personal roles in witness and ministry, the church permeates and penetrates its community in ways before impossible.

* reveals the latent energies and potential of the church. Its real course becomes clear when the whole fellowship participates.

And lay persons, insists John Havlik in *The Evangelistic Church,* are equal to the assignment. John Havlik writes, "The average layperson has a greater desire to be used in evangelism than church leaders realize . . . (but) laypersons require a great deal more help and equipping than most church leaders believe." [2]

The responsibility for training lay persons centers on the pastor. Tapping the unusual gifts and concerns of his church members can be among the pastor's most rewarding tasks. Even more important, developing lay persons' knowledge, interests, and talents will result in new freedom for the pastor and new life for the church.

When the people are integrated into the broad spectrum of membership responsibilities, concern for the church's well-being is mutually shared by staff and laity. As the whole church becomes truly the instrument of God, the fellowship of the redeemed, the minister of reconciliation to a pagan world, growth becomes an emphasis of the majority of church members, rather than the appointed few. The church's evangelistic methods and mechanics gain more diffuse scope.

And the bulk of church member activities are transferred from internalized housekeeping to external shopping, which results in seeking out those beyond the comfort of God's grace and drawing them into the warmth of his love.

Once a congregation has recognized its course of action, in fact, to fail to act can lead to pessimism and despair. People mature spiritually when they are given opportunity to determine where God wants them to work, then are able to walk through doors opened by the Holy Spirit. To hold them back, through indecision or timidity, causes frustration and dampens desire.

Empowered believers live not for self but for him who died and rose again. When they know who they are as individuals, who Christ is, and what his role is in their lives, and when they understand their relationship to the Father and all his children, they will exercise a faith worth of propagation.

One proven way to avoid such problems while building

total church involvement is through creation of an "Evangelism Leadership Group." In some denominations, this group is drawn from the church council, in others, it may come from regular committees or associations. However selected, these persons give leadership to church organizational programs and are, therefore, in position to fuse evangelistic concepts into all the activities of the church.

The group will study not only the functions of existing church organizations, but also the needs of the church's community. Their object will be to design a strategy which is consistent with the New Testament's vision of growing a church that fulfills Jesus' intent.*

Those enlisted as part of the Evangelism Leadership Group will become the nucleus of church growth. They, in turn, will help the pastor nurture church-growth concepts among the broad membership. As they are enlisted, and as they enlist others, they should measure their dedication against criteria necessary for the task.** Church growth leader Peter Wagner lists five such qualifications:

1. *Single-minded obedience.* Church growth leaders take the lordship of Jesus Christ very seriously. They have counted, as Dietrich Bonhoeffer would say, the cost of discipleship. They are willing to pay the price by doing whatever is necessary to obey and fulfill God's Great Commission.

2. *Clearly defined objectives.* Church growth leaders are motivated by the assurance that they have understood the revealed will of God for world evangelization and that they are attuned to what God expects to accomplish through them. Thus, they are not reluctant to set measurable goals and to allow their success or failure to be evaluated in the light of these goals, risky as this procedure might seem to

---

* See Appendix G for How to Form Evangelism Leadership Group
** See Appendix H for the Evangelism Leadership Group Commitment

some.

3. *Reliance on discerning research.* Church growth leaders are well aware of what must have been behind the words of Proverbs 18:13 (TLB), "What a shame—yes, how stupid!—to decide before knowing the facts!" All too often Christian work is undertaken ignorantly simply because the facts of the situation are not adequately known.

4. *Ruthlessness in evaluating results.* Church growth leaders have often been criticized as being too pragmatic. They are pragmatic, (but) they would like to consider it as *consecrated* pragmatism. If methods currently being used for some evangelistic effort, for example, are not accomplishing the stated goals, they must be revised or scrapped. A strategy must be substituted that will produce the results that God desires.

5. *An attitude of optimism and faith.* Church growth leaders are not intimidated by the charge that they are "triumphalists." They are convinced that Christ is building his churches as he said he would (see Matthew 16:18), and they are confident that the gates of hell will not prevail against it. They are excited about participating in the building of the church worldwide and they rejoice when churches grow and multiply.[3]

Church members willing to accept such stringent criteria will be open, caring, and evangelistic to everyone. They will never be part of a church built on exclusiveness in regard to wealth, race, social status, or age.

They will, as was expressed in a litany given in a church recently, experience a "wave of light breaking into the darkness and a voice saying, 'You are accepted.' "

Leader: Simply accept the fact that you are accepted.

People: If this happens to us, we experience grace.

After such an experience, we may not be better than before, and we may not believe more than before, but everything is transformed.

Leader: In that moment, grace conquers sin, and reconciliation bridges the gap of estrangement. We perceive the power of grace in relation to others and to ourselves.

People: And we experience the grace of being able to look frankly into the eyes of another—the miraculous grace of reunion of life with life.

Christians swept up in this spirit of salvation through grace cannot help but be part of an all-sharing community, they give as has been freely given. Their churches do not continue to feed on themselves, do not baptize their own alone, and are not faced with a painful, protracted death by attrition.

For the reunion of life with life offers, in the example of Christian witness, a church whose "I's" are ever on the future.

Notes

[1] Elton Trueblood, *The Incendiary Fellowship,* (New York: Harper and Row, Publishers, Incorporated, 1967), p. 31.

[2] Havlik, *The Evangelistic Church,* p. 15.

[3] Wagner, *Your Church Can Grow,* pp. 30–32.

"And He gave some as apostles, and some as prophets, and some as evangelists, and some as pastors and teachers, for the equipping of the saints for the work of service, to the building up of the body of Christ; until we all attain to the unity of the faith, and of the knowledge of the Son of God, to a mature man, to the measure of the stature which belongs to the fulness of Christ. As a result, we are no longer to be children, tossed here and there by waves, and carried about by every wind of doctrine, by the trickery of men, by craftiness in deceitful scheming; but speaking the truth in love, we are to grow up in all aspects into Him, who is the head, even Christ, from whom the whole body, being fitted and held together by that which every joint supplies, according to the proper working of each individual part, causes the growth of the body for the building up of itself in love" (Eph. 4:11–16, NASB).

News Item 7

CLARKSDALE, MISS.—Emphasizing traditional church programs and untraditional attitudes of love and acceptance, James Sanders has jarred rural New Hope Baptist Church from static dead center to a real high spirit of growth and outreach.

Since coming two years ago to this small church, eight miles south of Meridian, Sanders has seen attendance jump in all areas of church life:

* Sunday School has increased from an average of less than 150 to more than 225;

* Church training has jumped from "none when I came" to more than 100 each Sunday night;

* worship services have climbed from less than 200 to more than 300 every Sunday;

* choir membership has more than doubled.

For an open country church, Sanders said, "This is really something. But it's not because of me. The Lord has been dealing with it."

Sanders came to Clarksdale, a tiny community with only the county school and a general store, from a stable, secure Mobile, Alabama, pastorate. To come he had to take a cut in salary and live in a smaller parsonage.

But Sanders believed "I'm not the type to evangelize the city, but to tend the sheep in a rural setting like this. I've always felt my calling not so much as an evangelist but as a pastor."

When he arrived at New Hope the church was at low ebb, "The stewardship program was slack, the missions concern was nil, the Sunday School was very down. The Lord has taken all this and turned it around," Sanders concluded.

Growth began almost immediately. Aided by a steady trickle of newcomers—Meridianites moving out from the city—the church turned around its downward trend.

"But," Sanders emphasized, "the growth was not all transfers of letters. About half of those who have joined have come by baptism," he said. And the church has attracted all ages, from youth to senior adults.

To help spur growth, Sanders tried twice to institute a visitation program. "It didn't go," he admitted. But he and members of various Sunday School classes visit regularly.

In fact, Sanders has strongly pushed Sunday School and other traditional church programs. "If you can build your Sunday School," he pointed out, "you can build the church. In Church Training and Sunday School, we study and learn how we can minister to others."

Revivals, special meetings, and celebrity speakers/preachers have not been part of New Hope's growth. The key has been the atmosphere of warmth, love, and acceptance that permeates the 130-year-old church.

"My philosophy is just to love the people," he explained. "I don't preach down to them, I just let them know I'm human. I'm not above them, but with them.

"We don't question people about their past, we just try to accept them as they are and build on that."

When newcomers began moving into the old, rural community, some tensions flared between them and the church's longtime members. But the conflict between old ideas and new ones was quickly quelled as the people saw Christianity as love.

"I preach love and teach love and try to love. I think this attitude is catching. The people have grown in love. They love the Lord and others around them. When that happens, you're naturally going to be faithful to what the Lord commanded. And you're going to grow."

7 | Process (1):
Fitting System to Strategy

In church life, methods should be consistent with the essential nature of the fellowship. Methods express character, and not only the character of persons who compose the church, but the character of the church itself.

When the church's methods—its organizations and superficial activities—substitute for the core task of sharing the life of Christ, the character of church members and their church is out of sync with the New Testament example.

Missionary Melvin Hodges has said, "Methods are no better than the men behind them, and men are no better than their contact with God. We can study methods of church growth and write books about indigenous church principles, all of which is well and good; but we will never have anything like New Testament churches and New Testament growth until we get something like New Testament men (and women) with New Testament experience." [1]

Too often, a method, once accepted, is never evaluated or assessed again. Churches waste time defending methods when they should be defining Christ. Rather than exploring what the Spirit is saying in the life of the church, the pastor and/or lay persons slide along in a business-as-usual syndrome. "Methods like committees can multiply until they become accretions," warns Myron Augsburger, "and like barnacles on a boat may not only retard its [(a church's)] progress but result in its ruin." [2]

Church growth needs to speak to the renewal of structures and forms. The present shape of congregational experience may hinder growth, structure may prohibit the Spirit's work.

Perhaps the first rule of church growth is that no methods are sacrosanct. Every activity should be evaluated in light of current needs and future plans. Every program should be examined to determine its viability and use as an instrument of church growth.

Vitality and newness should pervade all church actions. When programs become sluggish or outdated, when problems are discovered—whether lack of interest or ineffectiveness—change is in order. For programs and structures are to serve people, not be served by people.

However, a word of caution, the old "baby-with-the-bath-water" adage is true, change for the sake of change is not wise. Implementation of church growth strategy will inevitably involve some existing church programs. Each has the capability of contributing to the total mission of the church, the question is, do they? And perhaps more important, do they contribute in a manner that gives maximum impetus to the church's overall purpose?

Dissecting the dynamics of growth are difficult, because no actions occur in a vacuum, the processes of determining and defining growth objectives overlap with certain events happening almost simultaneously. But every church, no matter how large or small, goes through stages as it attempts to unite its people in common strategy.

Already, pastor and church staff—however large—have studied together the theology of the church's mission and attempted to define positions and priorities. Results of the study should be written down, from a clear, precise, and simple statement of purpose to an exhaustive list of community needs and opportunities.

Key lay leadership, such as the Evangelism Leadership Group, has also begun preparatory steps by studying, with pastor or staff, the nature of the universal church and the potential of their local congregation. Their deliberations, from discussion of purpose to implementation of goals, should also be written out.*

Once pastor, staff, and key lay persons are united in goal and direction, they move to share their vision with the

---

* Refer to Appendixes A, B, C, D, E

entire congregation.

Churches have used different methods to accomplish this. One Atlanta church, faced with the problem of evangelism in a neighborhood threatened by racial transition, began its formal preparation with a series of retreats for key lay people. Pastor and staff discussed their concepts and understandings of the biblical imperative of blind missions. Once responsible lay leadership had captured the pastor's vision, they, in turn, began a series of Bible studies that involved almost the entire church. At the same time, the pastor delivered a series of sermons on the subject.

The neighborhood changed, the church integrated. It lost members, but growth continued. It serves its community still, even though today its community is racially different.

Fortunately, few churches have to hammer out their concepts against such tense racial backdrops. Yet every church does have to work through the same procedures to be able to assess intelligently its current work and future guidelines. And every church must do so with the same sense of urgency that moved the Atlanta church. Only then can the church be ready to act, not react, to bring its community to Christ.

Many churches have found a special Vision Month emphasis seriously involves laity in designing structure and programs that further growth goals. If it earnestly seeks to draw pastor and lay people together in common objectives, Vision Month can be a helpful emphasis.

Vision Month should be directed by the pastor and the evangelism leadership group. From their studies of community needs and church opportunities, the special churchwide focus can be developed.

The first week of Vision Month centers on discovery and understanding of the leadership group's findings and the pastor's biblical insights. The second week explores ways to meet these needs and commandments. The third week involves personal commitment of both leadership and laity to the possibilities discovered. Here the church calls for individual commitment to God's will "for my life and for my part in his will for my church."

At every phase, responsible leaders share their vision with the congregation and discussion is encouraged. Teachers, both in classes and in small groups, evolve their ideals. Youth are asked for their insights and given a chance to catch the vision of the adults. Every segment of the church is saturated with enthusiasm and excitement, until the entire fellowship soaks up the desire to fulfill God's will through all means available.

The fourth week of Vision Month is Vision Week. Testimonies are shared as the entire congregation focuses on priorities being considered for the church. Sunday climaxes the month's emphasis. In the morning service, the people are challenged to respond to the developed goals and action plans. That evening in a Vision Commitment Service the people are given an opportunity to become an integral part of making the vision come alive.

Once commitments are made, the remaining business is to begin the processes of growth. Administratively and organizationally, the puzzle fits together to make a concentrated whole. And the church, its every action to this point permeated by prayer, becomes more than the sum of its parts.

The traditional Sunday School or Bible study program is the first important element to consider. The greater a person's exposure to Bible study, the greater his or her commitment.

When people come together to learn God's Word and attempt to apply it to their own lives, a cross-pollination occurs that enlarges and extends individual insight.

Because Bible study enriches lives, churches have found it to be a significant method of reaching people in need. It is not surprising, therefore, that Sunday School has become, for most churches, the largest organizational program and a major source of new church members.

Statisticians estimate Sunday Schools peak in attendance at approximately 55 percent of their enrollment. Consequently, a church wanting to grow will find it advantageous to increase Sunday School enrollment.

Some churches have ceased to stress adult Sunday School. Their morning Bible study activity has become geared to children and youth. This is a mistake that not only shortchanges adults who need Bible study to mature as Christians, but also handicaps the church's growth. Every Bible study class provides the believer with an opportunity to witness! Points out religious education specialist Gaines S. Dobbins, "To teach without leading unsaved members of the class toward Christ and to Christ would be like the farmer planting seeds and failing to harvest the crop."

Visitation is a natural part of any Sunday School program. Family members recommend other family members, friends recommend friends, the circle expands until the church touches many lives in the community.

In the warmth of a close-knit group, individuals move through the stages of discipleship, their weaknesses made strong by the fellowship shared, their Christian outlook matured in the context of common goals reached by the class.

Arthur Flake, a leader in Sunday Bible study development, listed five steps in "building a standard Sunday School" that are viable for churches seeking to grow through this program. The steps are:

1. Find the people.
2. Provide space.
3. Train leadership.
4. Enlarge the organization.
5. Divide and multiply.

Sunday School programs that do this will be effective tools in feeding prospects into the worship services of the church. Most important, however, they will develop individuals who can witness to their faith. A laity equipped to witness can give dramatic impetus to the coming of the kingdom here on earth.

Many churches also have programs of Church Training development. In the Southern Baptist Convention, the purpose of Church Training is to assist churches in establishing, enlarging, and improving the biblical understanding of church members. Church Training attempts to help Christians apply Christian teachings to their everyday lives.

Especially important are four emphases of Church Training:

1. Train in church leadership.
2. Deal with family life.
3. Equip through church doctrines.
4. Equip for evangelism.

For both Sunday School and Church Training, much literature has been developed to assist churches in beginning and conducting these programs. Valuable materials and projects for outreach are available from most denominations. There is, therefore, no excuse for a church, serious about growing, not to take advantage of these helps.

Men's and women's organizations also exist in most churches. Often these are designed to support the missionary efforts of the denomination. This is a worthy goal; their prayers and monetary support are needed by those "especially called for missions." But their task does not end with praying and giving.

All who have been redeemed share a common purpose which is spreading the gospel to others. Personal mission-action is the responsibility of every believer. No Christian, of either sex, legitimately can avoid "the confrontation between individuals in which one verbally represents to another the gospel message, including the need for personal acceptance of that message."

To grow a church seeking to fulfill its mission, men's and

women's organizations must encourage their members to participate in a life-style of evangelism. They must train their members to seek out witnessing opportunities. They must help define church strategy and support it in their words and deeds.

The men's and women's organizations are usually sensitive to persons of special needs or circumstances. To these, the organizations must be able to give the gospel along with the cup of cold water. (Yet they should never use their concern for a person's physical needs to manipulate him or her into a spiritual decision.)

One of the most vital roles for both men's and women's organizations comes as the church develops its plans for growth; their support during the process of awakening can be critical to the success of any projects that come later.

The men's and women's organizations, because they usually develop a close fellowship, also provide an environment for renewal, so significant in any church wanting to grow. A group of men and women, having experienced renewal, can create a climate of meaningful participation that will envelop the entire church and anchor the total strategy of concern for and promotion of church growth.

A final organization found in most churches is the church choirs. Church music has, in fact, a strong opportunity for witness because it gives individuals a chance to personally express the joy and hope of their faith in a manner that does not seem blatant or offensive.

Music obviously enhances congregational worship. It provides a dynamic, emotional outlet for personal witness. It offers a warm, sensitive atmosphere in which individuals can make conversion decisions. And it can give depth and life to what might otherwise be a cold and unfeeling experience.

But this is only the traditional aspect of a church music program. Today's skilled church choirs have opportunities to sing on television, in shopping centers, at festivals, and fairs. In such places, their contemporary sound can testify to their biblical faith. Their witness can be as forceful as it is entertaining. The Southern Baptist Convention, for example, uses hundreds of choir-tour groups each summer in its mission outreach efforts. Estimates are that these groups sing before thousands of non-Christians each year, many of whom would have no other exposure to the gospel message. The number of persons who have made commitments to Christ as a result of these groups' performances can only be guessed, but Southern Baptist leaders believe they contributed significantly to the denomination's continued and outstanding church growth during the past ten years.

Other churches may have other organizations or programs. As with those mentioned above, the phase-one effort of any church growth plan is to evaluate what exists and revamp, remodel or jettison as needed. The system must fit the strategy. When system and strategy mesh, church growth occurs.

Unfortunately, the doubts that caused anxiety over failure to grow seldom arise when the church's structures are functioning as effectively as they should be. When a church's growth slows or dies, it is often because its level of program and organizational output is insufficient. In normal times, rejuvenation of these programs might be adequate to reverse trends.

But on other occasions, the church has dipped too low. Something must be done to supplement existing programs. But what? Where does the church turn when it seeks a new horizon of growth?

Notes

[1] McGavran, Guy, Hodges, and Nida, *Church Growth and Christian Mission,* p. 32.

[2] Augsburger, *Invitation to Discipleship,* p. 91.

"You, however, continue in the things you have learned and become convinced of, knowing from whom you have learned them; and that from childhood you have known the sacred writings which are able to give you the wisdom that leads to salvation through faith which is in Christ Jesus. All Scripture is inspired by God and profitable for teaching, for reproof, for correction, for training in righteousness; that the man of God may be adequate, equipped for every good work" (2 Tim. 13:14–17, NASB).

"Now the God of peace, who brought up from the dead the great Shepherd of the sheep through the blood of the eternal covenant, even Jesus our Lord, equip you in every good thing to do His will, working in us that which is pleasing in His sight, through Jesus Christ, to whom be the glory forever and ever. Amen" (Heb. 13:20–21, NASB).

News Item 8

JENNINGS, LA.—In this heart of Cajun French territory, Catholics and Baptists are finding renewal of lay persons the key to church growth.

First Baptist, a static congregation of 700 members, on an eighteen-year downhill slide, held a lay renewal emphasis during the summer of 1975.

The meeting had "the best attendance of any we've had since I've been here," said five-year pastor Lawrence Baylot. More than 450 people were sitting on top of each other in a church building that holds only about 350 on Sundays.

"Our people were excited by the prospect of involvement," Baylot explained. "We have a celebration of discovery, of *koinonia*. We gained new hope, new openness, a new willingness to share.

"Lay involvement," he added, "is the key to the future. The laity isn't listening to the professional clergy, it's listening to others who walk their walk. Lay renewal is the only thing I see encouraging right now," Baylot continued.

Eighteen months later, Baylot sponsored a second renewal event. Emotions and commitments of the first experience jelled on this occasion. Baylot said, "People realized they've been called to be participants in ministry."

A number of ministries have, in fact, been germinated by the events. "I tried to get them into a position to discover how God can use them," Baylot said, "but our lay persons have started the ministries on their own. I've had nothing to do with it."

Church members started two Bible studies. One attracts thirty women each week, the other, begun by an eighty-year-old member, draws nine-to-ten elderly people in a housing development.

A paraplegic member, who discovered he had gifts despite his handicaps, counsels and teaches Bible in a convalescent home.

An extension ministry takes worship services and whatever else is needed to homes of shut-ins. "Whether they're red, yellow, black, or white, we try to minister to their spiritual and physical needs," Baylot said.

Yet all of this has not upped church attendance, Baylot admitted. It has, however, created a climate in which growth can occur—for the first time in years. "We're on step toward growth," Baylot indicated. "Statistically, we're not there. But we're moving there."

More than that, Baylot said, the church's new enthusiasm has been catching in this small community. The local minister's association, of which Baylot is president, has nurtured a great spirit of cooperation among churches of all denominations.

"We try to be honest and open with each other. We share what's happening in our churches," Baylot said. "We take hands and pray together."

When Baylot began telling of his church's renewal experiences, the Catholic priest, Ronald Groth, took an interest. Young and evangelistic, Groth asked Baylot to share renewal procedures with his laity.

Baylot, Groth, and the local bishop met. The Catholic leaders supported Baylot's belief that renewal could not occur if the Catholics did not accept the priesthood of the believer. When they explained Vatican II had given new importance to lay participation, and that they felt a focus on gifts of the ministry was essential for rejuvenating their own congregations, Baylot agreed to lead a renewal conference for them.

Some sixty deeply committed Baptists and more than 450 equally dedicated Catholic Christians then met for an event whose excitement still lingers in the community, Baylot said.

"If I could have the ministry in my church I have down the street (at the Catholic church)," Baylot commented, smiling, "it would be great. It's wild what has happened."

A second meeting is planned to continue the emphasis.

Meanwhile, conservative, tradition-bound Jennings—a community static in population and resistant to new ideas—is being exposed to both Catholics and Baptists becoming alive and active.

"Spontaneous things are happening," Baylot said. "People are becoming committed. I believe there's a flood coming," he concluded, "and I can hardly wait."

8 | Process (2):
Awaking, Equipping, Developing

Only when the church proclaims the gospel to its community can it be called the church. Consequently, any "come to church" emphasis must be coupled with a "go and witness" thrust.

Whenever the "come-go" balance is upset, the church faces slow death by attrition. And the only remedy is to recreate the atmosphere which nurtures personal spiritual growth while encouraging personal witness development.

If traditional methods fail to infuse the desired vitality into a sleepy congregation, church leaders must recognize the need for "spiritual awakening."

A spiritual awakening is an experience of the congregation in which the reality of what God is doing through his Spirit fills the people. They are refreshed by a saturating awareness of the presence of God, and they are enthused by a new and deeper interpersonal relationship with other believers; they are empowered by the Holy Spirit.

Bold acts of witness result when a congregation translates the teaching of Christ into life-style. Paul explained the result of his awakening experience to the church at Corinth: "And my speech and my preaching *was* not with enticing words of man's wisdom, but in demonstration of the Spirit and of power: That your faith should not stand in the wisdom of men, but in the power of God" (1 Cor. 2:4–5).

Resistance and hesitancy are swept aside, and a new creative tension develops in the congregation. Old ways and old outlooks struggle against the fully comprehended meaning of Christ's good news. Now clearly understood, the cost of grace—of living Christ's redemptive ministry—is weighed against the drowsy ease of lukewarm church membership.

But for the church truly awakened, the fact that God's

people are set free to *be* the good news through a dynamic life-style witness signals the end of self-concern, self-worry, self-motivation.

Spiritually awakened and empowered, believers exercise their gifts in witness and ministry. They literally gather to be scattered. Their lives and words demonstrate the good news: because Jesus is Lord, they are liberated to discover and develop their God-given human potential.

United in the fellowship of Christ, believers face personal responsibilities with renewed determination. In tune with God and in close relation to each other, they seek a style and commitment to become the functioning body of Christ. Dynamic spiritual growth patterns develop in a people sensitive to the will and mind of Christ. Ministries flow from the abundant joy and overflowing desire to share Christ's love with others.

But spiritual awakening cannot be ordered like pizza, with free home delivery. God uses many avenues to bring in a churchwide renewal experience. However, all avenues require congregational work, planning, prayer, and dedication.

The benefits of spiritual awakening are many; but the costs are high. For different people respond to different actions, and the church may have to develop a whole series of events in order to catapult the entire congregation into new life.

Local church revivals or crusades are one way. Sometimes families who express minimal concern for spiritual things are turned on as a result of the excitement these events offer others. Sometimes the freshness of an outside speaker, or the inspiration of newly prepared musical performances, will touch a person's life.

Development of discipleship groups and groups focusing on witness-growth activities are other ways to stimulate a churchwide spiritual awakening. Under mature leadership, group experiences often bring a person into a keener understanding of God's will for his life. Through study of

God's Word, prayer, and a renewed search for God's presence in every aspect of life, a person may gain insight into his opportunities of service.

A renewal event is another way. In many churches, lay renewal weekends are catalytic experiences which give people a new awareness of God and his plan for their lives. Calling lay persons into an open expression of their faith develops close ties with others who, in like faith, wish to make a clear witness.

Certainly God uses unstructured and spontaneous ways to awaken his people. Particular experiences—a word from another person, a message from the minister, a Bible study in a home, or a prayer meeting—can be the catalyst for a spiritual awakening.

Occasionally, too, activities designed for equipping believers catch them at a time when they are especially sensitive to the workings of the Holy Spirit. Such events as a lay evangelism school or Sunday School teachers' training session may yield more than dry recitation of equipping practices.

Since church leadership should continuously be about the business of equipping the saints, every training event could also be seen as a renewal event, as well as an opportunity to affirm the gifts and abilities of each church member.

The apostle Paul, the first church-growth specialist, pointed out that God "Gave some as apostles, and some as prophets, and some as evangelists, and some as pastors and teachers, for the equipping of the saints for the work of service to the building up of the body of Christ" (Eph. 4:11–12, NASB).

The word equipped translates a Greek word from which we get the English noun, artisan. An artisan is a craftsman, someone who works with his hands to build or make things. This word appears in the New Testament only in Ephesians 4:12, but other forms of it are found in Matthew 4:21 and Galatians 6:1. In Galatians, the word expresses the idea of "mending." In Matthew, it is used as a term for "prepare for action."

The people of the church are, therefore, to be shaped, mended, and prepared. The purpose is building up the church and fulfilling the ministry of witness.

Any church that neglects its equipping ministry surely limits its growth potential.

Church growth will not move at a rapid pace until the people are equipped to do the job. And carelessly scheduled, or poorly planned events are not adequate to train believers. Training is not simply book knowledge or how to do something, it is a working knowledge that involves individual practice.

All persons of the church should possess witnessing skills. The manifestation of these may be in varied forms, from street witnessing to teaching literacy. Some may actually communicate Christ's gospel nonverbally. But the Great Commission is clear: all followers are to go into the world and express the good news *in some way* that is natural to their gifts and abilities.

The believer probably will not—perhaps cannot—do the work of the church on mission unless he or she is equipped by the church to do so. Missionary Roland Allen says, "It is the training of the first converts which sets the type for the future. If the first converts are taught to depend upon the missionary, if all work, evangelistic, educational, or social is concentrated in his hands, the infant community learns to rest passively upon the man from whom they receive their first insight into the Gospel." [1]

"Growing churches evangelize unbelievers," agrees John Havlik, "nurture believers, start new churches, and encourage and motivate youth to accept Christ's challenge to professional careers in growing evangelistic churches around the world." [2]

The church has the responsibility to equip as part of its process of nurturing believers. "Education has been called a controlled process of growth," writes Paul Benjamin.

"Physical and spiritual growth requires time. An equipping minister who is well acquainted with the congregation has knowledge about his gifts and capabilities about people. His task is to assist them in climbing the stairway of Christian responsibility. Together they are both liberated to carry out the ministry of Christ." [3]

The equipping process releases persons to express their own uniqueness, rather than molding them into Christian automatons while killing their imagination and initiative. Only those who apply what they learn can travel the road of high adventure for Christ.

Equipping can be done through mass media training of large numbers; through small-group techniques; or on a personalized, one-to-one basis.

The mass approach, probably the least effective, is most often used in churches. It is a valid approach, used by para-church groups for years. Some denominations, such as Southern Baptists, have developed excellent programs which use mass involvement but also break large groups into smaller units for more personalized training.

The Southern Baptist lay evangelism schools—sometimes called "Witness Involvement Now"—have, for example, been responsible for training thousands of lay persons in witnessing techniques.

The small group, popular today in many churches, takes advantage of fellowship relationships that can develop among a few people meeting together with a common spiritual emphasis. Jesus himself used this method when he trained the twelve. Research indicates members of small groups retain more of their training than those in large groups, where superficiality may be necessary.

One-to-one training can be a most effective and extensive means of witness training, but it is also the most time-consuming. Its advantage may come in the intensity of the personal relationship. A trainer can pour himself into the student. If the student catches the dedication and commitment of the teacher, he may be able to share this with others. A chain of student-trainer relationships can develop that are strong in outreach potential, because no weak links have been welded into the process.

The pastor, of course, as the initial teacher, must remain sensitive to the particular personalities, characteristics, and needs of his people. Their level of Christian experience will determine the kind of training and equipping approaches to be used. Always the process should be flexible and open-ended, however, leaving room for creativity and individual expression.

It should be, also, cyclical. Spiritual growth does not stop with a new members' orientation class, a lay evangelism school, or a renewal weekend. Each day, each week, each year, Christians must mature spiritually, as well as physically. Becoming a Christian is never a finished task, it is a lifelong process. One of the beauties of the Christian faith is that it is never complete or finally understood by any believer, but continually surprises and delights believers with new truths and new revelations as they move from one stage of the Christian journey to the next.

For the church to experience significant numerical growth and for the believers in the fellowship of believers to fulfill their personal responsibilities to Christ and to each other, the church must mature spiritually.

Objectives of spiritual development in believers include bringing glory to God, intensifying the desire to continue in the Christ-walk, and helping find avenues and natural ways of witnessing one's faith.

"Therefore," said Paul, "if any man is in Christ, he is a new creature; the old things passed away; behold, new things have come. Now all these things are from God, who reconciled us to Himself through Christ, and gave us the ministry of reconciliation" (2 Cor. 5:17–18, NASB).

The first task of the church may be to provide for those who are newborn into the family of God. Jesus said, "Teaching them to observe all things whatsoever I have commanded you" (Matt. 28:20). In Acts, Luke revealed that the new believers "Continued stedfastly in the apostles' doctrine and fellowship" (Acts 2:42). Follow-up of converts is, therefore, essential.

Individual counselor training at this point is excellent. Done by the pastor or someone designated by him, the personal relationship allows the new believer to see the meaning of Christ's message and the joy of spiritual thought through the acts and words of another Christian. As the counselor verbalizes his faith, the new Christian discovers ways to verbalize his. The human example gives life to Christ's teachings.

Other techniques for new believer follow-up include:

* orientation classes, which not only describe denominational polity and practices, but also emphasize the individual responsibility of each Christian to witness and minister. Opportunities for involvement in the local church's activities, plans, and projects should be part of the training session(s).

* witness-growth groups, which incorporate the new member in a fellowship of older members. Each group sets its agenda from those suggested by the pastor and/or church leadership. The new believer comes to discover his own link in the chain of witness and ministry.

* renewal weekends or retreats, which offer a natural continuance of the new birth experience. These can be times of significant growth in personal spiritual understanding as well as opportunities to discover personal gifts for ministry.

* lay equipping exercises, which provide practical training in techniques of witness and ministry.

But just as the new believer must be led toward spiritual maturity, so older members of the body of Christ must continue their development. Any church interested in growing should recognize the importance of continually providing events which expand horizons and explore new gospel ground. The concept of grace, for example, could involve Christians in a lifetime of study and contemplation. The practice of prayer, so vital to a Christian's closeness with God, will be exhausted as a subject of inquiry.

In these ways, Christians will mature, edging little by little toward their goal of becoming the world's yeast, salt, light. They will come to the church for the spiritual insights and truths it offers their lives. And they will go from the church renewed, invigorated, and challenged to spread the joy of Christ's good news and its meaning in their lives.

Theirs will be a positive, dynamic witness that undergirds and builds a growing church.

Notes

[1] Roland Allen, *Missionary Methods: St. Paul's or Ours,* (London: Lutterworth Press), p. 81.

[2] Havlik, *The Evangelistic Church,* p. 104.

[3] Quoted from prepublished manuscript copy of *The Growing Church* by Paul Benjamin.

"Be on the alert, stand firm in the faith, act like men, be strong. Let all that you do be done in love" (1 Cor. 16:13–14, NASB).

News Item 9

SILVER SPRING, MD.—Two years ago, David Kim announced over radio and in Korean newspapers that a Korean-language Baptist worship service would be held in a former Anglo Baptist church building here. Kim was surprised that almost 100 people came. Now those 100 have doubled, becoming fast-growing First Korean Baptist Church.

"For Koreans," explained Kim, "America is known as a Christian country. When they come here, they like to join a church where they can meet with their own folk and learn how to handle their new lives."

Although about 20,000 Koreans live in the Washington, D.C. area, only one-tenth of them attend a church of any kind. Most Koreans are from Buddhist or other Asian-religion backgrounds.

"Shifting from the traditional family religion to an evangelistic one entails a cultural transition that is difficult," said Danny Moon, Korean language specialist for the Southern Baptist Convention.

However, some Christian denominations, especially Presbyterians and Methodists, are highly evangelistic in their mission programs in Korea. So Koreans coming to the US do not find Christianity as "foreign" as do immigrants from some other Asian countries.

The cultural shock of their new environment can even aid in the effort to enlist new members in the church, Moon indicated.

"Koreans—as well as other ethnic groups in America—tend to band together to protect their cultural heritage," said Moon. "It's human nature to want to get together with men and women like ourselves."

When Pastor Kim first began Korean First Baptist Church in 1975, it was a mission sponsored by an Anglo congregation nearby.

In the early days, he spent 80 percent of his time, he said, helping new immigrants find jobs and homes. But as the church has grown, his duties as pastor have demanded more time.

To contribute to the community, the church does sponsor a day-care program for all children—Anglo and Korean, Kim said.

Kim said he has been pleased by the people's acceptance of the church, but he added that the scarcity of Korean-language materials—both for Bible study and for lay training—handicaps the church's continued growth.

Nevertheless, Kim has led his church to begin a Korean mission in neighboring Fairfax County, and has given up one of First Korean Baptist Church's members, Song Moon-Sup, to be its pastor.

It is this spirit of missions outreach that has led Korean Baptist churches to be among the fastest growing ethnic churches in the United States. In the past three years, thirty-four Korean churches were started, sixteen in 1975 alone.

For Pastor Kim, this is not enough.

"We would like to begin more Korean missions around Washington," he said. "We have three or four lay persons in our congregation who are interested in starting new work.

"I believe we must continue to reach out to where the people are," Kim concluded. "We must make the sacrifice of ourselves."

9 | Perils: Watch Your Step!

For the church to fulfill its mission with energy and effectiveness, it must be healthy. Its vital signs—growth, outreach, ministry—must reflect its tensile strength and its resilience against common church ailments—the messiah complex, the building syndrome, and the laity lethargy. Finally, like the body of Christ, it must grow both in size and maturity. The furious spurt of youth must be coupled with qualitative internal maturation, or the body will develop into a distorted, deformed being.

One of the most dangerous obstacles to church growth is the messiah complex that occasionally engulfs pastors who believe church growth evidences their own ability rather than an outpouring of the Holy Spirit.

The pastor is called of God. Charged with a scriptural mandate, he is to use his talents and skills for God. As a professional in his field, he is trained and ordained. He is the key person whom God uses to grow a fellowship of believers.

While this is his responsibility, he can abuse his leadership role if he allows his own agenda to replace God's, or if he allows the church to become a personality cult.

Such a pastor becomes captive to his own self-importance. Capriciously, with pride and haughtiness, he acts with more concern for the institutional church than with the kingdom of God. In the short run, church growth may occur. But growth will be ephemeral and soon, cliques will develop and the fellowship will disintegrate, turning into a house of numbers without harmony.

As dangerous as the autocratic leader is, the pastor who is so insecure, so unsure of his own abilities that he is incapable of exercising leadership is even worse. His actions sometimes come across as laziness, leaving the church apathetic toward growth. Filled with its pastor's no-care attitude, lay people limp along, their excitement dulled and potential stymied. At other times, the pastor's indecision results in a confused, directionless congregation. Inertia dampens the spirit of the fellowship and programs sink when launched.

It is possible, too, for a pastor to allow his dreams to run amuck with reality. Priorities must correspond with New Testament concepts, and they must match possibilities.

Some pastors leap on their horses and attempt to gallop off in all directions. The church without a serious strategy, clearly defined and continually enunciated, goes nowhere. Goals are meaningless unless they are set in the context of church size, location, membership, and potential.

Occasionally, pastors turn outside their congregation for help in setting goals and developing strategy. Counsel from Christian church-growth specialists is good. But to bring in a specialist for an event-oriented experience, such as a renewal retreat, is not a substitute for full, concerted, cooperative planning by the pastor and congregational leadership. Such an event is input into the decision-making process, it is *not* the decision-making process itself.

Activities of church growth are not confined to a few dramatic events or a pastor's strident shouts. Events may punctuate growth, giving it momentum or emphasis. But to rely on events for growth is an error in judgment. They are parts of the process, and are vital but not alone.

The pastor's drumbeats and "come-on" cries are tinkling cymbals and empty gongs unless given life by his personal motivation. Trial balloons are merely hot air. Congregations may be pumped up to the point of exploding, but church growth vanishes after the pinprick.

Author Hollis L. Green lists three motivational perils:

"(1) Push motivation—which uses fear as its force; (2) pull motivation—which uses incentives and rewards (as its force); (3) personal motivation by love.

"When Christians have to be pushed or pulled into participation or involvement in the program of the church, it should be obvious that something is wrong with both the program and the Christian." [1]

The effective pastor plans for church growth by involving his laity in all phases of the decision-making process. He carefully blends his roles of parent-teacher-energizer to bring out the best of his people's interests and ideas. He is aware of his own humanity, sensitive to his own frailties and weaknesses, as well as his capabilities and strengths. He is neither a workaholic nor a procrastinator.

And he seeks, in every opportunity, to climatize his congregation to the opportunity God gives his followers to live and work for him.

Climatizing evangelism, in fact, describes the process that involves the lay people on significant avenues of church development. When the atmosphere suggests a people working together in love and common cause, pet projects of pastor and/or laity will not sidetrack the church's movement. Projects and activities can be mercilessly scrutinized, those which have outlived their usefulness can be abandoned, those that contribute to growth can be perpetuated.

Says Hollis Green in *Why Churches Die,* "Church growth problems will persist as long as the church attempts to perpetuate programs that are complicated and ineffectual. The more difficult a program is to understand the fewer persons will be motivated by it." [2]

The major intent of the church can be thwarted when people, in their preoccupation with details of ongoing programs, forget the thrust of the task. Climatizing evangelism frees people from their all-consuming involvement in the minutiae of church life and sets their sights on the ultimate goals.

Climatizing evangelism unshackles dynamic lay leadership and develops positive influences to spur the church to a profound hopefulness in its fellowship and its community. An awareness of God's presence, an infusion of the inner warmth and inner compulsion of his will, invigorates the congregation. A people paled by previous patterns and unworkable programs take on the rosy-cheeked glow of health.

The church feels alive.

Unfortunately, such a spirit threatens some pastors. They tend to rely on a few workhorses whose actions they can control and trust, rather than develop the gifts of the full congregation. They fear serious exploration of the role of gifts as described in the New Testament, for such realized gifts can give rise to a strong laity—one not so easily circumscribed or controlled.

Certainly a laity split into dozens of omnidirectional factions can be disastrous to the fellowship. But this rarely occurs where the clergy gives unidirectional attention to the concern of church growth. Good, solid biblical teachings, and a proper interpretation of spiritual gifts for ministry, assists the pastor rather than hampers him. People find their places alongside him. It is, after all, better to have spirited, aggressive participation than none at all.

Some pastors, however, become so anxious to involve their members they fail to offer opportunities for adequate Christian development. Church growth may be occurring at such a rapid pace that the pastor grabs any warm body to keep from slowing momentum.

Paul warns against this, urging, "Do not lay hands upon any one too hastily and thus share responsiblity for the sins of others; keep yourself free from sin" (1 Tim. 5:22, NASB). He mentions duties of caring for untrained disciples.

German theologian Dietrich Bonhoeffer stresses the consequences of cheap grace. Easy, conciliatory approaches to reaching people produce converts; but these new believers may never be strong enough to stand alone, much less maintain a consistent Christian walk.

Numerical growth necessitates healthy spiritual care. Persons reached for Christ grow in an active Christian relationship. "The best way to do that," says evangelism professor Lewis Drummond, "is through the foundation of a new Christian orientation."

Drummond lists seven ingredients:

"1. A rooting and grounding in the salvation experience.

"2. An overall grasp of the great doctrines of the faith.

"3. An understanding of what the Bible is and how to read it profitably.

"4. A basic primer on prayer. (The convert learns to pray.)

"5. A vision of how Christ's victory is ours today and how to overcome obstacles.

"6. The role of the local church in a believer's life.

"7. The necessity of witnessing and service." [3]

Many church growth specialists emphasize the potential of growth offered new converts by fellowship circles, a concept which divides a large church into manageable levels of intimate relationships. Newcomers can get lost in the crowd, but their feelings of estrangement can be overcome by tying church members, new and old, together in fellowship circles which offer them friendship and nurture in Christian life patterns.

The exciting promise of such groupings can only be dimmed if they are allowed to become closed cliques. As long as the groups remain open to newcomers and flexible in their structure, however, this need not become a problem.

Fellowship circles functioning at their best are among several excellent ways of maturing the newly converted. Whatever the method, this is a constant demand. As Latin American theologian Orlando Costas has pointed out, "the perfecting is the province of Christian education. (But converting and perfecting) both are essential stages for effective church growth . . . . Evangelism and Christian education, discipling and perfecting, conversion and nurture, qualitative and quantitative growth—these are two inseparable dimensions of the process of growing in the

Lord. It is in the light of this process that church growth theory interprets the task of mission." [4]

"Each of the dimensions of growth—qualitative and quantitative—should be taking place together and interacting under the guidance of the Holy Spirit," adds another church growth specialist.

Immature Christians may have a high degree of enthusiasm, but a low degree of understanding. "The things which you have heard from me in the presence of many witnesses," says Paul, "these entrust to faithful men, who will be able to teach others also" (2 Tim. 2:2, NASB).

The church serious about growth will not run aground because it has failed to provide opportunities for Christians to mature. It will recognize that Christianity is not a point in time but a continuous process, a life-journey that begins with the new birth.

And just as Christians must change as they mature in their understandings of their responsibility in Christ, so too must churches change. Leadership must continually seek new vision, for a church without it is a closed shop, its people dedicated to internal concerns, oblivious to needs outside the walls.

Those with vision must articulate their dreams, enabling others to catch their excitement. The church is a community of thinkers and doers, both contributing their special gifts and abilities. When they work in unison, growth results.

But occasionally churches have members who feel their gifts make them more capable, and more worthy of recognition and leadership, superior to others in the fellowship. They want to dominate the church and, at times, the pastor. They may accuse the pastor of dictatorial conduct when he acts aggressively, yet, when given authority, they are more dogmatic than the pastor they criticize.

Not every pastor can or should be as blunt as one in Texas. He had been having a running battle with one member, who believed the pastor's leadership was leading in the wrong direction. The pastor finally called the woman to his study for a conference. When she arrived, he met her at the door. "Madam," he said, "this church is only big enough for one of us. I'm not leaving. Therefore, I believe you'll be happier elsewhere." She changed churches the following Sunday. The pastor remained with the church almost forty years.

His handling of the situation may not have been the best course of action, but he did evidence an understanding of those who abuse or misuse their positions and gifts to gain personal influence. Such people, he realized, can make life miserable for the entire congregation.

If they are not to disrupt the fellowship, their energies must be channeled into church growth plans. However pastor and/or church leadership decides to handle such people, their actions should reveal love, kindness, and wisdom from on high.

Such situations also can contain theological implications, in that differences arise as to what the church should be and do. Misunderstandings of the mission of the church can be clarified by New Testament theological studies, preaching and teaching. Efforts to involve laity and opportunities for discussion and feedback can help unify the congregation's conceptions of the nature and direction of the church.

Another theological concern revolves around the meaning of conversion and evangelism. When members of the congregation fail to recognize their personal responsibility for witness to the non-Christian people in the community, the sparks of evangelistic fervor are extinguished in the church.

Attitudes such as "we've enough churches," or "let someone else do it," dismiss the reality of hundreds in any community who attend no church. Because each individual should have the opportunity to experience the same joy and fellowship of belief in Christ, church members who shirk their responsibility turn their churches into exclusive clubs.

Such churches, their doors closed against the outside world, stagnate. Christ's church is *inclusive*. Christ's church is also people, not buildings. Too often, pastors and lay persons confuse erecting buildings with building a church. The size of the structure becomes symbolic of the congregation's greatness. Square feet are more important than their creative use, carpets and parking lots become goals and community need is lost in campaigns for a new steeple. The worth of the physical plant seems a more significant measure of success than the lives touched, ministered to, helped, and healed by the church's activity in the world.

That outlook reverses the Great Commission. "As you go . . ." turns into "as you come . . . ." The work of the church focuses on such phrases as:

"Come to Sunday services."

"Come to business meeting."

"Come to church fellowship."

"Come to hear our pastor."

"Come to enjoy our music."

"Come to bowl or play basketball."

"Come, come, come to our church . . . ."

All of the above are legitimate goals for the church, and they encourage people to come to God's house. But strategy based on "come" and not "go" soon degenerates to a shallow concept of "us four and no more."

Someday the fellowship will cease its growth because the church has limited itself to functions only at the church house. Beyond its walls, the world whirls along, unaware the church is playing a waiting game that requires the lost to know—literally—before the door opens.

Buildings were never part of New Testament church growth strategy. Today, nevertheless, many churches are crippled by a structure psychology that keeps them from functioning as house churches or home Bible fellowships, from meeting in Grange halls or storefront buildings, and from holding multiple services with staggered hours. For too many, bigger means better when it relates to acreage, not people.

Make no mistake, buildings are important. Churches need to support them and work to create places whose appearance enhances reverence and worship experiences. But when the majority of the church's budget goes to maintain buildings, or for new and more modern facilities, then the church has lost sight of its first goal and its first stewardship responsibility which is evangelism.

A church strategy based on a building mindset, come-to viewpoint misses the intent which God has for the church. It also parallels another problem area which is tenure. Older members often are reluctant to let newcomers assume positions of responsibility. "They don't understand the church. They haven't been here long enough" is an attitude that can cause tensions within the body. A wise pastor and leadership will create pluralism with a range of choices and opportunities for service for members at every stage of development.

A related problem deals with the church's relations with other churches, both within and outside its own denomination. Occasionally churches avoid opportunities for growth because they feel their actions might create tension with a neighboring church or within the local denominational association. Yet another church may decide to ignore its peers and grow in directions that cause disharmony.

Only application of New Testament principles can determine the correct course for a congregation, but more is at stake than mere numerical growth. The church exemplifies Christ here on earth. Its actions in its treatment of others will be judged by those outside its fellowship—both Christian and non-Christian.

To gain a reputation as a growing church may be worth whatever antagonism arises between churches or denominations. The sacrifice may result in a more dedicated, determined congregation. But that reputation may also be detrimental to the advancement of the kingdom.

Weighing such actions-reactions is difficult, but some questions include: Is our reason for church growth selfish? Is it to better another church? Is it vengeful? Is it a rebellion against the denomination? Is it out of a sense of arrogance? And, finally, is it shallow? Does it really purpose to recreate the body of Christ on earth? If so, does it represent more than outreach? Does it also seek to minister and to serve?

The church, says theologian Orlando Costas, is a sign of reconciliation. That means, he says, "that she must herself be a reconciled community. . . . Her message is a living testimony of the light which shines in the darkness and which the darkness cannot overcome. . . . To achieve this end, the church must dramatize and exemplify a genuine life of reconciliation by practicing love, justice, and peace in her own midst." [5]

The church which strives to be a growing church, a living, vital, vibrant church, is also a servant church. It shows its concerns for humankind in loving, sacrificial service. Ministries range from tutoring to clothing distribution, and actions create a climate of mercy, humility, justice for all persons. Programs are blind to race, economic level, and social status, but see clearly and seek to heal the hurts, frustrations, and discouragements of persons.

A one-dimensional church does not express the multifaceted personality of Christ. Concern for the conditions of an individual's spiritual condition must be paramount, but with it is concern for the conditions of an individual's physical existence. Both concerns are part of the church's mission and Christian's responsibility to offer abundant life.

The church that seeks to grow must also be willing to die. Churches that become overprotective of themselves cease to be living organisms and become stagnant institutions. Missions *is* also the goal of growth. A danger resulting from accelerated growth is self-centeredness. And a self-centered church may be unwilling to give the time, money—and people—necessary to begin other churches.

This is not New Testament!

To plant another fellowship in an area of need is a natural part of the reproductive process of growth. Churches seeking to fulfill their mission are mission-minded churches.

They are also, in the final analysis, churches that recognize with single-minded devotion the meaning of mission. Says Orlando Costas, "When church growth theorists affirm that the aim of evangelism is *the* multiplication of churches, they are advocating a theology that makes the church the end of God's mission. Granted that the gospel is community-oriented. The question is whether the community is the objective or a result (a necessary and imperative one) of the communication of the gospel. Or to put it in other terms, whether the community is an ultimate or a penultimate goal of God's mission." [6]

Churches which understand that distinction will be churches who experience growth that truly represents Christ's life and promise and hope for tomorrow.

Notes

[1] Hollis L. Green, *Why Churches Die*, (Minneapolis: Bethany Fellowship, Inc., Copyright 1972), p. 37. Used by permission.

[2] Ibid, p. 36.

[3] Drummond, *Leading Your Church in Evangelism*, p. 136.

[4] Costas, *The Church and Its Mission: A Shattering Critique in the Third World*, p. 112.

[5] Ibid, pp. 69–70.

[6] Ibid, p. 135.

"But you shall receive power when the Holy Spirit has come upon you; and you shall be My witnesses both in Jerusalem, and in all Judea and Samaria, and even to the remotest part of the earth" *(Acts 1:8, NASB).*

News Item 10

HAYWARD, CALIF.—Eight years ago, Charles Bennett was a mailman. Today he pastors one of the fastest growing churches in the Bay area—1,200-member Palma Ceia Baptist Church.

The transition from mailman to pastor wasn't easy for Bennett. Nor did it come quickly. But once "I believed the Lord wanted a church in Hayward, I didn't give up," Bennett said.

Although first feeling a call to preach in Ohio in 1945, Bennett "wouldn't answer until 1963," he admitted. He continued to deliver mail, preached whenever he could, and attended a Bible institute in Oakland at night for four years.

In 1965, Bennett felt led to begin services in Hayward, but his brother's death in Ohio postponed his action. "It took everything out of me," Bennett recalled.

Instead, Bennett joined a Southern Baptist church in Oakland, even though he had grown up in a National Baptist church. The decision proved significant, for in East Oakland Baptist Church, Bennett found encouragement and opportunities to exercise his leadership.

His three years there gave him training and exposed him to many programs available through the Southern Baptist Convention. "The Lord has a way of preparing his servants," Bennett said.

By 1968, Bennett could delay no longer. With only his family to preach to, he began services in Hayward, a middle-class, bayside community south of Oakland.

After three weeks, eight women with their children came to hear him. When he finished his message, he remembered, "I explained why I had come to Hayward and told all who wanted a church there to come stand with me." Already three black churches were in the city. Yet all but one woman came forward. And Palma Ceia Baptist Church was born.

From the first, Bennett stressed Sunday School. He had been a Sunday School superintendent at East Oakland, and he knew Sunday School was a good way not only to reach others, but also to help his members mature. Most of them, at this time, were women with children—and the children "needed Sunday School to help them in their lives," Bennett said.

He continued to deliver mail, visiting nights and weekends.

Until 1970, the church had grown only to 130 members. Less than 120 were attending regularly when the congregation moved from a rented Congregational building to its own facility.

More and more families visited, liked the friendly atmosphere, and joined. The snowball effect—so common among growing churches—developed. Growth created growth as the congregation became excited about the life and ministry of the church, Bennett explained. Attendance doubled, then tripled.

In the first four months of 1977, Bennett baptized fifty-six people. The church budget—which only had become strong enough in 1975 to allow him to quit his mailman job to become full-time pastor—will top $100,000 in 1977.

And the congregation, while still containing many divorcees and single people, shifted toward professional, middle-class families. So young did its median age become, in fact, that Bennett could not find enough low-income elderly in the church or the church's neighborhood to justify a "meals on wheels" program Palma Ceia wanted to cosponsor with the city.

He also began extensive "discipleship training" in thirteen-week sessions.

Two Sunday morning services soon were necessary. The main one at 11 A.M. has more than 500 packed in ever Sunday, the earlier service attracts half that number.

Weekday activities range from programs for women, youth, and children to the adult-oriented discipleship training. "You'd think we were having church, we have so many come," Bennett said. "We've got the strongest visitation and witness program of any black church in the Bay area . . . maybe any church, black or white," Bennett added.

That active lay witness program, plus what Bennett described as "the presence of the Holy Spirit, first of all, naturally," has been the cornerstone of Palma Ceia's growth, Bennett commented.

"I'm not a great preacher," he said, although most of his congregation deny that. "But I hope to be a great pastor and a great teacher of my people."

And the first lesson he's taught, for all the years of his pastorate, has been that there is "liberty in Christ." So open and accepting has become the atmosphere at Palma Ceia, that members drive fifteen to twenty miles one-way to attend.

"I wanted a feeling of Christlikeness," Bennett explained. "I didn't want people to feel like strangers at Palma Ceia, I wanted them to feel part of the family of God."

"At Palma Ceia," commented a white visitor recently, "everyone sure feels that!"

10 | Power: The Exciting Side of Pentecost

Filled with the Holy Spirit, the church presents the most powerful force in the world today.

Christ created the church and promised it the final victory. To enable the church, and to enable individual Christians, God sent the Holy Spirit. Throughout history, from Pentecost to the Great Awakening to the "Jesus Movement," whenever the Holy Spirit has surged in the hearts of God's people, new territory has been gained in the persistent struggle against evil.

For centuries, believers energized by the Spirit's presence have faced pagan and distraught communities. They performed miracles which evidenced the reality of Christ's lordship over the natural world. They taught with a skill that revealed Christ's command over the intellects of men and women.

At Pentecost this Spirit poured upon the church, fulfilling Christ's promise that the church would never be held in the shadows of time. Comforted and helped, strengthened and bolstered, Christ's followers turned from their desolation.

The Holy Spirit—the enabler—filled the vacuum left by Christ's departure. He gave early church members the encouragement they needed.

The Spirit became their teacher, giving them the fullness of knowledge. He entered the lives of sinful human beings, serving as the instrument of their conviction. He revealed evil natures, but also pointed the way to goodness and salvation. He became the sanctifier, maturing new believers in Christian growth and understanding.

The Spirit saturated the church with a corporate power, greater than the sum of its human parts, empowering the body of believers to mold a new world view from a hostile, gluttonous society.

The church today, 200 centuries later, has the assurance of the Spirit's continued work in its midst, turning feeble Christians into fearless examples of Christ's reconciling love.

Yet too many refuse to allow the Master's surge of energy to revolutionize their lives. Their greed or lust or pride or prejudice or vanity crowds out the Spirit. Their feculence when confronted by the world's pressures compromises the Spirit's power to break the chains of spiritual darkness and purify the mind.

Instead of opening their lives to the Spirit, they attempt to purchase success through human resources. It would be a blessed day for the church if every believer would stop his or her inefficient and fruitless service for the church. It would be better to wait to be empowered from on high.

The tragedy of this century, as in any other, is the person who stumbles along in church life without real spiritual energy, never understanding that the Holy Spirit is not a power a person uses, but a power which desires to use a person.

Theologian Lewis Drummond, in *Leading Your Church in Evangelism,* describes the nature and work of the Holy Spirit:

"(1) In the Holy Spirit we are set free from the law of sin and death (Romans 8:2).

"(2) In the Holy Spirit we are strengthened in the inward man (Ephesians 3:16).

"(3) In the Holy Spirit we find God's leading (Romans 8:14).

"(4) In the Holy Spirit we bear fruit (Galatians 5:22–23).

"(5) In the Holy Spirit we are led into all truth (John 16:13).

"(6) In the Holy Spirit we learn to pray effectively (Ephesians 6:18).

"(7) In the Holy Spirit we can communicate the truth to others (I Corinthians 2:15).

"(8) In the Holy Spirit we can evangelize in power (Acts

2:4–41)." [1]

Possession of the Holy Spirit does not give power, but a sense of indwelling and infilling that strengthens the inner person and enables a new nature. He permeates every experience, affecting the whole of life and coloring all actions and events. He renews, freeing the believer from control by fleshy interests. He creates in the believer an enjoyment of divine things that penetrates the whole being.

In Christ, the believer becomes a new creature, empowered by an inner relationship, sealed and directed and controlled by the indwelling Spirit of God.

Through that inward relationship with the Spirit, the believer fulfills his amenable life-style as a follower of Christ. Explains R. A. Torrey in *How to Obtain Fullness and Power:*

"The Holy Spirit is the person who imparts to the individual believer the power that belongs to God. This is the Holy Spirit's work in the believer, to take what belongs to God and make it ours. All the manifold power of God belongs to the children of God as their birthright in Christ . . . . To the extent that we understand and claim for ourselves the Holy Spirit's work, to that extent do we obtain for ourselves the fullness of power in the Christian life and service that God has provided for us in Christ." [2]

The vitality of the committed life flows into growth and maturation of Christian outlook. Fruits, not gifts, reveal the power of God in the veins of the believer. The Christian life-style expresses joy, love, peace, confidence, warmth, and concern for the human condition.

Jesus said, "When the Holy Spirit has come upon you; and you shall be My witnesses" (Acts 1:8, NASB). The Spirit gives vigor for bold witnessing; he grants strength for diligent service in ministry. Through him, lives and lips support each other, giving credence through actions, the verbal testimony. Not only do a Christian's words tell others that Jesus cares, his life also shows others that Jesus is alive and continuing to care.

"After all," says theologian Costas, "the gospel is not merely good news about a past event. It is this, of course, but it is also good news about a living person who is himself acting redemptively through his Spirit in the here-and-now." [3]

When individual Christians evidence, through the indwelling Spirit, that Christ is alive in them, the church becomes a reservoir of power. In corporate witness, the church shows to the world a people unified in the Spirit.

The joy of the Christian fellowship is a magnetic attraction in a world of sorrow and pain. Aware of its inescapable challenge to be the body of Christ, it becomes a cleansing, healing tide that washes its community. As individuals linked by common cords, the church stands as a bulwark in turbulent times, a haven of rest for the weary, a hope for the hopeless, and a comfort for those who need the touch of a warm hand.

Energy radiates from the fellowship of believers. Through their acts of love, the outside community discovers the vitality of their commitment. With peace, gentleness, and goodness, God's people reflect a corporate relationship that is other worldly.

Cleansed of selfishness, of prejudice, or narrowness, and in liberty by grace, the Spirit-filled church lunges forward. In thought, word, and deed it reveals for everyone an infectiously joyful existence. Its amazing and heavenly peace in the presence of shame, suffering, and death offers an anchor in today's stormy seas.

The joy of God's power is the music the church sings, the love of God's sacrifice is the poem the church writes in the lives of its members.

Fellowship, loyalty, understanding, and unity of purpose are as normal in believers as breathing. Genuine communion with God is not only an individual experience, but also part of the corporate expression.

One who cares brings others to God in petition, recognizing that Jesus Christ on the right hand of the Father, hears and intercedes. Paul says even the Holy Spirit carries our prayers to the Father.

In its study of God's Word, the corporate fellowship discovers power. The truth erupts out of each word, clarifying life's purposes and revealing how Christians should relate to each other and to the world in all its tumult.

Biblical authority undergirds individual and church action; it also becomes the funnel through which believers find God in the events of history; the writings of present-day authors; the lives of dozens of persons, living and dead.

Scripture answers questions of God's holiness, sovereignty, and majesty. At the same time, it determines humankinds' relation to him. Although human finiteness keeps humans from ever fully understanding infinite God, they may discover in his Word enough revelation to allow them to shed the skin of their old humanity for a beautiful, thrilling new nature which grows through generative maturity.

In the corporate fellowship of the Spirit, believers share victories and defeats, they lean upon each other. They find solace in the community's warmth of trust and love. In the disclosure of what God is doing in the life of one, all are strengthened.

Church growth, therefore, will probably never fulfill God's purpose unless the people absorb the presence of the Holy Spirit. He gives the power to look beyond self to the multitudes who have never experienced the abundant life. He lifts the church's eyes toward a horizon of commitment to humankind.

As the men and women of the New Testament age went to conquer their world, so must the church today. They were outnumbered, persecuted, forbidden to preach, and finally killed. But their commitment to Christ's ideal world sent them, sustained and infused by the Holy Spirit, on a one-way pilgrimage.

Today we live on the most exciting side of Pentecost. The church can grow; stripped of burdensome racial bias, cleansed of culturized religious tradition, purged of corrupted theology, and directed from above and impelled from within, the church can strike a resilient cord in the heart of humankind.

The nature of the gospel demands witnessing, discipleship, and ministry—the people of God, under the indwelling, sovereign spirit of Christ, can penetrate society's shell, everywhere sharing, preaching, teaching, and caring.

The people of God can become the living good news.

Notes

[1] Drummond, *Leading Your Church in Evangelism,* p. 155.

[2] R. A. Torrey, *How to Obtain Fullness of Power,* (London: Lakeland Paperbacks, 1955), p. 31.

[3] Costas, *The Church and Its Mission: A Shattering Critique in the Third World,* p. 191.

"So the church throughout all Judea and Galilee and Samaria enjoyed peace, being built up; and, going on in the fear of the Lord and in the comfort of the Holy Spirit, it continued to increase" (Acts 9:31, NASB).

"And they were continually devoting themselves to the apostles' teaching and to fellowship, to the breaking of bread and to prayer. And everyone kept feeling a sense of awe; and many wonders and signs were taking place through the apostles. And all those who had believed were together, and had all things in common; and they began selling their property and possessions, and were sharing them with all, as anyone might have need. And day by day continuing with one mind in the temple, and breaking bread from house to house, they were taking their meals together with gladness and sincerity of heart, praising God, and having favor with all the people. And the Lord was adding to their number day by day those who were being saved" (Acts 2:42–47, NASB).

11 | Product: The Dream Come True

"I want my church to grow!" Church growth is not easy. But it is possible. Not among those who are pessimistic or filled with despair, not among those who blame our times and hide their failures behind extenuating circumstances, and not among those who see reasons as excuses or opportunities as obstacles.

"I want my church to grow." The process is difficult, demanding corporate efforts of pastor and laity and Holy Spirit. Yet work and prayer can turn those simple words into the exciting proclamation: "My church is growing!"

And that is God's intent. For an alive, vibrant church evidences the characteristics first described in Acts:

"So the church throughout all Judea and Galilee and Samaria enjoyed peace, being built up; and, going on in the fear of the Lord and in the comfort of the Holy Spirit, it continued to increase" (Acts 9:31, NASB).

That striking word-picture could be written on the lintel of any forward moving church in any era.

Note the specific characteristics: harmony ("enjoyed peace") . . . spiritual development ("being built up") . . . reverence ("going on in the fear of the Lord") . . . strength ("in the comfort of the Holy Spirit"). The result? *Growth* ("continued to increase").

Although the passage refers to the full body of believers in that entire region of the world, it can be applied equally to local assemblies who meet together today in the name of the Lord Jesus. It describes the life and nature of the group of people who work at fulfilling God's purpose for their existence.

At peace . . .

In the Acts account, the reference was to past happenings. Bitter persecution had occurred, Saul of Tarsus had heavily attacked Christians. Then, following his miraculous conversion, he had become a serious disciple of Jesus Christ and the major church growth strategist of the New Testament.

Consequently, the churches enjoyed rest and peace, and grew in harmony. The first disciples "day by day continued with one mind . . . They were of one accord having all things common" (Acts 2:44–46). Like skilled violinists sensitively playing in harmony, the early church knew no discordant notes to grind the nerves and disrupt the concord of the fellowship.

The growing church has little time to allow quibbling among its members. Under God's control, church members encourage and strengthen each other. Individual faults are not stumbling blocks in a fellowship filled with love and harmony.

With spiritual development . . .

Like harmony, spiritual growth results when churches begin to grow. When the church is strengthened and consolidated, it matures. Individuals move along the course of discipleship, their commitments deepening, and their understandings growing.

In old believers' lives, new believers find models— imperfect reflections of Christ, yet people whose witness, Scripture identification, prayer, and regular service for others in Christ's name sets examples for others progressing along the road to robust, virile Christian adulthood.

As family after family come into the circle of fellowship, the church is filled with inexpressible joy. As family after family moves along their Christian journey toward healthy, dedicated fellowship, the church is cloaked in expressible hope.

The vision of growth becomes the victory of growth.

In reverence . . .

A third expression of a growing church is reverence for God. Walking in the fear of the Lord clearly interprets walking with a deep understanding of and consequent reverence for God's presence among his people.

Fearing God is not to shrink in apprehension, it is to act bravely, but in humility, in love, and in obedience. Because God's people long to keep his commandments, their concern is to please him. Walking in reverential awe of his hand upon them expresses their awareness of his penetration of their lives.

Growth evidences God's special touch on a fellowship of believers. Strengthened by his presence, they act—recognizing that all they do, and all that happens, does not come from their own power, but from his power working in their lives.

People imbued with God's presence do not wish to disappoint or doubt or dishonor him. Their praises are expressed in the reverential reality of him in their midst.

The spiritual strength . . . walking in the comfort of the Spirit is a significant mark of the productive church. No church has deep spiritual worth if it is not under the mastery of the Holy Spirit. No person, not even the pastor or church officers, can control the church fellowship, always the Holy Spirit is preeminent.

Such a church body depends not on methods, organizations, or programs, but upon the one who guides and controls every step of its growth. Church members do not merely talk of the doctrines of faithful service, but practice them while they go about their life relationships in shops, offices, businesses, factories, schools, homes. Their lives are testimonies to the joys of the Christian pilgrimage.

The congregation builds joy through Christ and matures in his grace. All aspects of the Christ's work on earth are expressed in actions of believers.

Luke describes how the early church multiplied when "All the believers continued together in close fellowship . . . Every day they continued to meet as a group in the Temple and they had their meals together in their homes, eating the food with glad and humble hearts, praising God and enjoying the good will of all the people. And every day the Lord added to their group those who were being saved" (Acts 2:44–47, TEV).

That passage reveals much more than the simple fact that churches were growing. It evidences the startling truth that in Christ, individuals were crossing cultural lines and religious barriers. They were proving that through his way, his truth, and his life all people wherever they are, whatever their calling, can become the heirs of God.

The first church people carried the gospel into the marketplace, spreading its message to neighbors, friends, strangers, enemies. They witnessed God's reconciling love to everyone they met.

Today's church people must repeat the first-century example. If they do, they will find no greater happiness than that which comes when persons are willingly used of God to reach those who do not know God, whose lives are outside the sheltering influence of his love.

Mobilizing the congregation to such involvement produces energetic evangelism. In a loving, tender way, people are confronted with Christ's demands. They are offered opportunities for accepting his salvation. They are turned toward the new experience of growth inside his will.

The job of the church is soul-seeking and soul-saving. When the church is not doing these two things, it misses the joy of seeing Christ's intent for persons fulfilled.

The growing church is vibrant, dynamic. Its productive characteristics include peace, spiritual development, reverence, strength, growth. Every church should reflect these as it accepts its mission and charges upon the world to accomplish it.

And, sensitive to God's promise and the presence of the Holy Spirit, every church should grow. If it truly believes, "I want my church to grow!"

Appendix A
Biblical Perspectives

Throughout this book we have made reference, again and again, to the biblical principles from which we draw the process and work described as "growing an evangelistic church." No congregation will find it possible to talk about church growth without founding its discussion on a solid biblical base.

Foremost among the pastor/congregation's questions should be: why are we here? what does God purpose for our particular fellowship?

Not every church will find the same answers. But the effectiveness of any programs or plans developed from the church's answers will be determined by the thoroughness of their biblical study together.

A basic outline for stimulating discussion is listed below:

1. *Growth is God's will.* The Bible teaches spiritual and numeral growth as a New Testament principle for both the individual and the corporate body (2 Pet. 3:18; 1 Pet. 2:2; 2 Thess. 1:3; and Eph. 4:13).

2. *The Great Commission stresses evangelistic growth.* Jesus made the winning of converts the heart of his charge to his disciples. He illustrated his concern for the evangelization of all people with the parable of the great supper (Luke 14:16–24). The close of the Great Commission suggests that this process ought to continue to the end of time (Matt. 28:19–20).

3. *Acts of the Apostles reveals the full scope of evangelistic potential.* The book of Acts is a description of the beginnings of the church. Under the motivation and direction of the Holy Spirit, it springs forward in an evangelistic surge. The church, spiritually, is a people whose community growth occurs not only under the guidance of the Holy Spirit, but also because the people courageously work in the midst of the world (Acts 2:42–47). They were continually spreading the good news of the gospel in the temple, in homes, and in the street. "Those who were scattered went about preaching the word" (Acts 8:4).

4. *The apostle Paul was an example of the growing activity* of an evangelistically concerned church starter, missionary (Acts 16). He envisioned the local church as a growing organism. He knew the responsibility of witnessing, winning, and maturing as he started churches across the Roman empire (Eph. 1:22–23; 4:1–12).

Appendix B
Purpose and Mission of the Church

Why does the church exist? Why are we here? Where are we going? What is our purpose in being? What is the mission of the church? What is the biblical base of the church? Answers to these questions that are biblical, Spirit-led, and relevant to the current church situation are very important in a church realizing what God wants to do in and through that church.

Framing the Statement

The goal is not to pinpoint isolated resource data to support an established point of view but rather to honestly seek a fresh assessment of the church and its purpose or mission. The data chosen for study should be assigned to members of the Evangelism Leadership Group for individual study. Each member should diligently study his assignment and reduce data to pertinent concepts and ideas. At a specified session, through discussion and reflections, the group should pull together the major insights gained from the study of the suggested resource data.

Two elements are essential in framing the statement: (a) beliefs and attitudes in relation to mission and (b) writing the statement.

(a) *Beliefs and Attitudes*

Even in a brief, working statement, we must face the following questions:

1. What do we believe about the nature of God? What are the implications for our actions?

2. What is our understanding of our own nature as individual human beings? What are the implications of this for the church and its mission?

3. What is our understanding of man as a social being? What are the implications of this for mission?

4. How do we understand the church as the people of God and as a human social institution? What are the implications of this?

5. How do we assess what our contemporaries see to be the major needs and issues? What are the implications of this?

(b) *Writing the Statement*

A final step in developing a statement for purpose or mission is to write the statement. This step requires much discipline but is most essential. In general, the statement should be brief and concise (one paragraph) yet not too general, it should also be clear and understandable, not vague and filled with religious cliches. The following form is suggested:

The purpose or mission of _____

(Name of Church)

is _____

_____

_____

_____

_____

Appendix C
Self-study Guide for Church and Community

1. What's happening in your church community?
   (1) Population: What has been happening to your population over the past ten years? the next ten years?
   (2) Age: Who lives in your community?

_____ under 5	_____ 20–24
_____ 5–9	_____ 25–34
_____ 10–14	_____ 35–64
_____ 15–19	_____ 65 or over

   (3) Race:

_____ White	_____ Black
_____ Spanish Language	_____ Other (___)

   (4) Occupation:

_____ Professional	_____ Laborer
_____ Manager	_____ Farm Worker
_____ Sales	_____ Services Worker
_____ Clerical	_____ Student
_____ Craftsman	_____ Unemployed
_____ Operative	_____ Retired

   (5) Marital Status:

_____ Single	_____ Separated
_____ Married	_____ Widowed
_____ Divorced	

   (6) Education:
   _____ Elementary through 8th grade
   _____ High school, 9th–11th grade
   _____ High school graduate
   _____ College, 1–3 years
   _____ College graduate

   (7) Family income:

_____ less than $5,000	_____ $10,000–$14,999
_____ $5,000–$6,999	_____ $15,000–$24,999
_____ $7,000–$9,999	_____ $25,000 or over

   (8) Housing:

_____ Renters	_____ Apartments, 2–4 units
_____ Owners	_____ Apartments, 5–49 units
_____ Single family	_____ Apartments, 50 or more units

(9) Future trends: What trends are projected that will affect your community? transportation lines? zoning changes? new buildings? redevelopment plans? housing development?

2. What's happening in your church?

   (1) Sunday School attendance: What's the average Sunday School attendance over the past ten years?

Average	Year	Average	Year

   (2) Baptisms: What were the number of baptisms for the past ten years?

Number	Year	Number	Year

   (3) Receipts: What were the total receipts for the congregation over the past ten years?

Number	Year	Number	Year

   (4) New members by letter: How many new members have joined the congregation by letter over the past ten years?

Number	Year	Number	Year

   (5) Open fellowship circles: How many fellowship circles are open in the congregation? List at least six formal groups, (Sunday School class, deacons, committee, music). What year were they formed?

Group	Year	Group	Year

How many members of the church joined the congregation during the past three years? _____ church council? _____ How many Sunday School teachers? _____ How many deacons? _____

How many members of the adult choir? _____ youth choir? _____

(6) Goals: What were the goals that were set for the congregation last year? This year? What are the accomplishments?

(7) Facility: Does your church facility communicate a positive image to the community? Is it structured to fit the needs of a growing congregation?

3. How can you get community and church together?

    (1) Use interviews with members: Interview key members and fringe members of the congregation (from youth to older adults). Use the following questions:

        (a) Why are you a member of this church?

        (b) What image do you have of the church?

        (c) What is the congregation's greatest strength(s)?

        (d) What is the congregation's greatest need?

        (e) If you could change one thing, what would it be?

        (f) What new ministries or programs would you be interested in being a part of at the church?

    (2) Use interviews with members, nonmembers, and community people asking what "image" they have about the church.

    (3) Use interviews with community resource personnel such as county or regional planning commission, county extension agent, land developers, education administrators, HEW, and utility company officials to try to gain insight into the following areas:

        (a) Where will future population growth be?

        (b) What kind of new industry is expected?

        (c) What do land developers plan?

        (d) Will newcomers be professional, blue-collar, low-income, or what?

        (e) Does it look like social or cultural characteristics of the community will be changing?

        (f) Will new families be young, middle-aged, or older?

        (g) Will new housing be low cost, moderate or high priced?

        (h) Will educational levels be similar or slightly different, greatly different?

    (4) Develop a community-church profile. Does your church membership profile match your community profile? What target groups of people are missing? List them:

What resources (strengths) do you have to meet these needs? List them:

_____

_____

What other resources are available to you to help reach these people? Denominational, community, and fellow churches in association:

_____

_____

Appendix D
Church Analysis

An adequate church analysis will assist in assimilating and presenting statistics of the church. Trends may be evaluated with conclusions which point to specific needs in programs and actions.

Two profiles for the church are provided for suggested use. The first deals with the physical makeup.

Suggested method for using the questionnaires:

Questionnaires for the physical and spiritual profiles can be administered through the Sunday School and Bible teaching organization(s). The following general instructions will clarify use of the questionnaires. Each should be taken on different days with adequate explanation of their purpose. If a church does not have a strong Bible teaching program, the beginning or ending of the worship service is the ideal time (to get a comprehensive survey the questionnaires could be used for those missing in the Bible teaching hour).

1. Give the questionnaire during the Sunday School assembly time or when the Bible teaching groups meet.
2. Give each person who is sixteen years of age or older a copy of the questionnaire.
3. Encourage total participation in the filling out of the questionnaire (one's own interpretation in every blank).
4. Specify that no name be on the questionnaire.
5. Allow ten minutes for them to complete the questionnaire.
6. Turn in all the questionnaires with the records or as soon as completed.
7. Keep all questionnaires separate by departments.

Tabulations from the questionnaires will provide a church profile to compare with the community profile. In addition, church member opinions will be recorded and can help the church leadership understand the commitment of the church to reaching out to people who have spiritual needs.

Appendix D(a)
Physical Profile

1. Sex: _____ male _____ female
2. Race: _____ White _____ Black _____ Spanish
   _____ Other (_____)
3. Occupation: (If more than one job, check all that apply)
   _____ Professional (doctor, teacher, technician, lawyer, artist, accountant, engineer, scientist, etc.)
   _____ Manager (manager, administrator, bank officer, business director, self-employed, etc.)
   _____ Sales (sales worker, clerk, advertiser, underwriter, insurance agent, etc.)
   _____ Clerical (bookkeeper, secretary, stenographer, typist, bank teller, postal clerk, cashier, etc.)
   _____ Craftsman (foreman, mechanic, machinist, repairman, carpenter, baker, etc.)
   _____ Operative or Transport (assembler, inspector, packer, butcher, garage worker, truck driver, bus driver, etc.)
   _____ Laborer (construction, freight handler, warehouseman, etc.)
   _____ Farm Worker
   _____ Service worker (policeman, health worker, child care, barber, teacher aide, private household, cleaning, food, etc.)
   _____ Student
   _____ Housewife
   _____ Part-time: _____
   _____ Unemployed
   _____ Retired
4. Age (check appropriate age bracket):
   _____ 16–19 years _____ 35–64 years
   _____ 20–24 years _____ 65 or over
   _____ 25–34 years
5. Marital status:
   _____ Single _____ Married _____ Separated
   _____ Widowed _____ Divorced
6. If you are a woman and have children under sixteen years of age, place the number of children in the appropriate age and sex bracket:

Female		Male	
_____	0–5	_____	0–5
_____	6–10	_____	6–10
_____	11–15	_____	11–15

7. Check highest educational level you have achieved:

_____ elementary, grade 1–4 _____ high school, grade 12

_____ elementary, grade 5–7 _____ trade school

_____ elementary, grade 8 _____ college, 1–3 years

_____ high school, grade 9–11 _____ college, 4 or more years

8. How long have you been a member of this church:

_____ less than 1 year _____ 6–9 years

_____ 1–2 years _____ 10–19 years

_____ 3–5 years _____ 20 or more years

9. Check all the following that influenced you or led you to join this church:

_____ Born into church

_____ Came on my own

_____ Friends recommended it

_____ Church's advertisement (sign, newspaper, yellow pages, etc.)

_____ Radio or TV ministry

_____ Former pastor recommended it

_____ A letter or printed material from the church

_____ Personal visit of the pastor

_____ Personal visit of a member

_____ Contacted through a religious survey, census, or canvass

_____ Backyard Bible club

_____ Revival/crusade

_____ Bus visitor

_____ Because it is my denominational preference

_____ We liked the worship services

_____ It is located near my home

_____ Spouse was already a member

_____ Because of my children

_____ We liked the minister

_____ It is a friendly church

_____ It is my family church (relative belongs here)

_____ Its program (music, education, recreation, etc.)

_____ Its facilities

_____ We share a common interest and background with the people of this church

CHECK IF YOU ARE ONE OF THE FOLLOWING:

_____ The head of your household

_____ The spouse of the head of your household *and* your husband/wife is not present to fill out a questionnaire

_____ Single, *and* not living with your parents

_____ Single, working full-time, *and* living with parents

ANSWER THE FOLLOWING QUESTIONS *ONLY IF* YOU CHECKED ONE OF THE ABOVE:

10. Where would you place your family income:

    _____ less than $5,000   _____ $10,000 to $14,999

    _____ $5,000 to $6,999   _____ $15,000 to $24,999

    _____ $7,000 to $9,999   _____ $25,000 or over

11. Residence: _____ own (buying) _____ rent (leasing)

12. Type of housing:

    _____ single family

    _____ apartment/condominium with 2–4 units

    _____ apartment/condominium with 5–49 units

    _____ apartment/condominium with 50 or more units

13. How long has your family lived at your present address:

    _____ less than 2 years   _____ 10–19 years

    _____ 2–5 years   _____ 20 years or more

    _____ 6–9 years

14. Approximately how far do you live from the church building:

    _____ less than 1 mile   _____ 6–10 miles

    _____ 1–3 miles   _____ 11–19 miles

    _____ 4–5 miles   _____ over 20 miles

15. How many persons are in your household: _____

16. Have you always lived in this state? _____ yes _____ no

    in this city? _____ yes _____ no

Appendix D(b)
Spiritual Profile

Please check the appropriate box:

	Yes	No	Uncertain
1. I believe every Christian should be a witness.	( )	( )	( )
2. I think we should try some new ways to worship.	( )	( )	( )
3. I pray with family or friends regularly.	( )	( )	( )
4. I believe planning is important to the future of the church.	( )	( )	( )
5. Watching television programs is an important daily activity for me.	( )	( )	( )
6. I have some close friends who are not Christians.	( )	( )	( )
7. I would like to see persons of other races or cultures active in our church family.	( )	( )	( )
8. I believe our church buildings are attractive to people driving by or walking by.	( )	( )	( )
9. I really do feel that I am getting the spiritual food I need from our worship services.	( )	( )	( )
10. I talk to people about Jesus Christ quite often.	( )	( )	( )
11. I have envisioned some things for our church that have come to pass.	( )	( )	( )
12. I really think a person's religion is his business.	( )	( )	( )
13. I feel older adults have unique needs which our church can help meet.	( )	( )	( )
14. I have found people in the church my greatest help when I have problems.	( )	( )	( )

15. I would really enjoy some ( ) ( ) ( )
leadership training.

*16. I believe that we should ( ) ( ) ( )
continue to support our TV
program because it is an effective ministry.

17. I think we pay pastors and ( ) ( ) ( )
staff to do religious work.

18. In the last three months, I ( ) ( ) ( )
have participated in a prayer
or Bible study group (exclud-
ing Sunday or Wednesday
church activities).

19. Are the church signs posted ( ) ( ) ( )
around the buildings in-
formative and appealing
to the general public?

20. I really feel a part of my ( ) ( ) ( )
Sunday School/Bible
teaching group.

21. I think ministering to the ( ) ( ) ( )
community outside the
church is very important.

22. I believe most people on ( ) ( ) ( )
welfare are lazy and need
to go to work.

23. I believe that people can ( ) ( ) ( )
lead a happy and fulfilled
life, though single.

24. I believe that some people ( ) ( ) ( )
have become inactive because
they have not been made to
feel a part of a small group
in our church.

25. I am willing to pay the ( ) ( ) ( )
price of change in order
to see our church continue
as an effective institution
in our city.

---

*A similar question concerning a ministry unique to the church being surveyed may be substituted if this is inappropriate.

Appendix E
Goals

1. Goals should be measurable. Be specific enough to determine capable accomplishment. Specify time to be accomplished.
2. Goals should be manageable. Each goal to be effective should be reasonable and within the scope of management by the group or church making it.
3. Goals should be relevant. They should relate to need to be met and to the situation in which they are stated.
4. Goals should be personal. The goal-makers should feel ownership. Each person assisting in making goals should feel he is personal and is accountable for his accomplishment.
5. Goals should be significant. Goals should have a balance between being reasonable and being significant to be challenging. Think in terms not only of what man can do but what God can do through man to accomplish challenging goals.

This work sheet is suggested for use in setting goals. Note the provision to list the needs, priority ranking, and writing out the statement of goal for each need. There may be need for more than one goal for each priority.

WORK SHEET
FOR
SETTING GOALS ON CHURCH GROWTH

Consider each need and its priority and then state a goal(s) for each. (There may be one or more goals for each need or priority.)

NEED: _____

_____

PRIORITY RANKING: _____
GOAL: _____

_____

_____

NEED: _____

_____

PRIORITY RANKING: _____
GOAL: _____

_____

_____

NEED: _____

_____

PRIORITY RANKING: _____
GOAL: _____

_____

_____

This work sheet may be reproduced for use by the group or the information may be listed on a chalkboard.

Appendix F
Pastor's Personal Commitment

The pastor who recognizes the exhausting nature of his commitment to church growth might wish to make a covenant with his congregation, so that they, too, understand the nature of the task being undertaken. Following is one such covenant possibility:

"I have studied carefully the biblical responsibilities given to me from the New Testament. I have developed a vision for growing a great church. I believe that God wants the church to grow both numerically and in a loving Christlike evangelistic ministry. Believing this, I make the following spiritual, intellectual, emotional, and physical commitment of myself to God and to growing a great evangelistic church:

(1) I commit myself to be a witness as my life-style and to develop my own personal spiritual life through prayer, Bible study, and meditation.

(2) I commit myself to continuing Bible study and prayer for feeding the flock of God.

(3) I commit myself to a growing understanding of the theology-vision of growing an evangelistic church.

(4) I commit myself to sharing the vision with individuals and groups within the church until the body of the church is permeated with a philosophy of evangelistic growth.

(5) I commit myself to enlist and involve an evangelism leadership group to implement growing an evangelistic church.

(6) I commit myself to the administrative oversight of equipping the saints to do the work of ministry as the pastor-equipper of the church."

_____

(Signed)

_____

(Date)

Appendix G
Evangelism Leadership Group

Southern Baptists in their strategy, *Growing an Evangelistic Church,* describe the formation of the Evangelism Leadership Group:

1. *Purpose of the Group*
   A. These leaders share with the pastor in a study of the theology of evangelism and church growth. They dream with the pastor and share his burden of finding God's purpose for themselves and their church in the community.
      The small fellowship of sensitive leaders experience exciting possibilities for what the church can become.
   B. The whole church shapes an entire picture of the total purpose of God. While they are representative of the whole church, their number is suggested from the following chart based on average Sunday morning Bible school attendance.
   C. The group supports the pastor as he moves beyond the creative atmosphere of this dreaming group. He senses being spiritually undergirded in a common dream with those who go to the church.
   D. Together the pastor and the entire group face each other, share with each other in the spiritual, theological and vision study as to what God wants to do in the midst of the fellowship. They draw together in agreement for the common goal, seeking the fulfillment of the will of God through the Holy Spirit. There is no hidden agenda with them. They become visionaries ready to move through the entire church body to develop and share the vision they believe has been given them by the Holy Spirit.
2. *Personnel of the Group*
   A. Leadership qualities should be considered prior to a selection of the council or group to assist the pastor in a broad involvement of the people.
      (1) The leaders selected should be warmhearted and open to God's leadership.
      (2) They must be influential and natural leaders in the congregation. They may not have an elected office but people listen to them and follow them.
      (3) They should be made up of both the "old-timers" and those who have paid for their recognition with faithfulness and loyalty through the years. It is well to use new people who have shown themselves in the congregation.

(4) They feel a strong relational tie to one another as well as the need to do the organizational work necessary to fulfill an involvement of the people. Their relationships evidence warmth of love and fellowship which can be "caught" by the whole congregation.

(5) It may be well to select several people who could be potential members with the option of dropping out when they see the in-depth study of the group.

B. A wise pastor will surely give consideration to use of groups who are already in existence.

(1) The pastor would be wise to use his church council or the elected leaders of the programs and organizations of the church. (However, these should be open and responsive to the open agenda concept.) Should these leaders be used, other representatives of the church ought to be added, such as young people, women, and whatever other groups who would give a total representation of the entire body.

(2) The deacons, if a church has deacons, or a similar type officer of the church could well be used if the church council does not wish to be used. However, if the deacons or similarly elected officials of the church are to make up the group, an invitation to as many youth and women should also be added for balance as with the council.

(3) When the church has a multiple staff of at least more than one, an involvement of these ought to be the first agenda of the pastor. He will work through the entire process of church growth and the mission of the church with the staff before the leadership group is formed. Their commitment to the full scope of church growth is as necessary as involvement of the people.

Appendix H
Evangelism Leadership Group Commitment

Those who become members of the Evangelism Leadership Group may wish to make a public commitment to the pastor and to themselves.

A suggested group commitment, to be signed by each member, is given below:

My personal commitment to growing my church:

I have studied carefully the theology and vision for growing an evangelistic church. I believe that God wants our church to grow both numerically and in the loving Christlike evangelistic ministry. Believing this, I make the following physical, emotional, intellectual, and spiritual commitment of myself to God and to growing this church.

1. I commit myself to be a witness in my life-style and to develop my own personal spiritual life through prayer, Bible study, and meditation.

2. I commit myself to a growing understanding of the theology and vision for growing Christ's church.

3. I commit myself to sharing the vision with individuals and groups within the church until the body of the church is permeated with a philosophy of church growth.

_____ Signed

_____ Date

The Evangelism Leadership Group will exchange this commitment page with other members of the group, and each person will sign as a commitment to one another.

Pastor _____   _____
        _____   _____
        _____   _____
        _____   _____
        _____   _____
        _____   _____